MW00876691

FREESTYLE
Competitive Swimming
Drills

Improve Technique | Add Variety
For Coaches | For Teachers | For Swimmers
Containing Over 100 FREESTYLE Drills

Second edition published in the United Kingdom 2020
Copyright © Eatsleepswimcoach

https://eatsleepswimcoach.com

Contents

Welcome

A very warm welcome to 'Freestyle Competitive Swimming Drills'.

About this publication
This publication provides coaches, teachers and swimmers with a series of tried and tested competitive freestyle swimming drills.
• These can be easily incorporated and adapted into your training or teaching programmes, whether you coach or teach rookie or national swimmers.

Delivering the technical demands of our sport
Competitive swimming can be a gruelling sport, requiring swimmers to undertake many hours of repetitive training each week, in pursuit of excellence.
• Developing a training or teaching programme that delivers the technical demands of our sport, while at the same time adding variety your sessions can be an ongoing process.
• This can be both difficult and time-consuming to achieve.
• Training or teaching programmes without fresh stimuli are in real danger of demotivating both swimmers, coaches and teachers alike.
• Over the past twenty-five plus years as a head coach, coach and teacher, I have managed to collate a large portfolio of competitive freestyle drills.
• I have used these to develop many young competitive freestyle swimmers from club to county, regional/state and national levels, the best of which are published here.

Publication focus

This publication focuses on the stroke's key technical areas.
● Each has its dedicated chapter, breaking down the stroke into its key constituent parts, to help both the coach, teacher and the swimmer develop and maintain a great freestyle stroke.

About Us - EatSleepSwimCoach

EatSleepSwimCoach is a competitive swimming website.
● Our team includes swimmers, swimming parents, teachers and coaches.
● With over 50 years of combined competitive swimming experience, both in the pool and open water.
● We provide swimming advice, drills, exercises, hacks, insight and tips.
● We produce publications, posts, articles and digital downloads on a wide range of swimming subjects.
● These include stroke technique, training drills and how to optimise training and competitive performance.
For further information please visit our website by using the following link: https://eatsleepswimcoach.com/

Facebook Group

EatSleepSwimCoach administers the **Competitive Swimming Exchange** Facebook Group.
● This is a competitive swimming group to help exchange ideas and information to collectively improve the sport we love.
● It's an international group for all swimmers, coaches, teachers, masters, triathletes and swimming parents.
● In fact, it's for all those who are interested in competitive swimming, either in the pool or in open water
For further information about joining this group please use the following   link: https://www.facebook.com/groups/thecompetitiveswimmingexchange

Coaching an Introduction

Competitive swimming training
Competitive swimming training requires the swimmer to perform repetitive technical drills, to master a set of key skills.
● This enables them to perform to the best of their ability, when under the pressure of competition.
● Repetitive training enables the swimmer to adapt their training to their 'muscle memory'*, enabling them to automatically perform as taught during competition.
*(*muscle memory - the ability to reproduce a movement without conscious thought, acquired as a result of frequent repetition of that movement)*

● If the training is repetitively performed with a perfect technique, then the muscle memory will store the perfect technique.
● However, if the training is repetitively performed with a poor technique, then the muscle memory will store this poor technique.
● Once a poor technique has been stored, this can be very difficult to correct.
● For any coach or teacher, it is important that they 'consistently and persistently' incorporate perfectly performed drills into their training or teaching programmes to reinforce and develop a great butterfly technique.

Swimming drills
I introduce drills into every training session.
● I incorporate them into every warm-up routine.
● I also conduct a twenty-minute 'drills activity after the warm-up,

before the swimmers become fatigued.
- I have found this is long enough to teach drills correctly and short enough for swimmers to maintain focus.

Make progress slowly
I have found that it pays to be patient when introducing a new drill.
- Some swimmers quickly learn some techniques and struggle to learn others.
- Coaches and teachers should use multiple coaching and teaching formats.
- Some swimmers may prefer to learn via verbal or written communication.
- Other swimmers may prefer to learn via a physical demonstration.
- Wherever possible, I use swimmers who have mastered a technique to demonstrate specific drills.
- I have found that using a senior swimmer to demonstrate drills to junior swimmers, is a very effective way of getting my coaching points across.

Only once a good technique has been mastered should the level of difficulty be gradually increased.
- These drills can be adopted and developed accordingly, by increasing the distance, intensity or decreasing the target time.

Training aids
Resistance, assistance and variety can also be added by the introduction of training aids such as:
- Bungee cords
- Drag belts/shorts
- Hand paddles
- Kickboards
- Pull buoys
- Snorkels
- Swim fins

Safety First
- Always ensure the safety of the swimmers in your charge, whilst carrying out any drill.
- Whether starting in the water or from a dive, please ensure your swimmers have enough room to allow the correct and unhurried execution of the drill.
- When starting any drill that requires a dive, please ensure the

swimmer can perform a racing dive safely and they have achieved the relevant competitive start accreditation.

Please note the drills contained in this publication are performed in a 25m pool.
• Please make the relevant adjustments if you coach or teach in a pool of a different distance.

I hope you find this publication useful, enjoy your coaching and teaching.

Coach Arthur

Chapter 1: Freestyle an Introduction

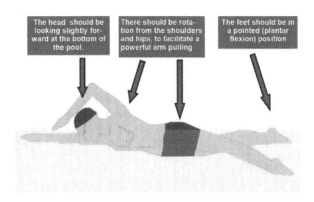

Freestyle is the fastest competitive stroke.
● Also known as front crawl, freestyle is used as the main fitness development stroke in most swimming training programmes.
● It is also the preferred stroke of most competitive triathletes and open water swimmers.

The correct position for an effective freestyle

Body position
● The swimmer's body should be in a prone (face-down), horizontal and streamlined position.
● This helps to reduce drag and establishes the correct platform from which an effective arm stroke and leg kick can be performed.

Head position
● The head should be in the water whilst not breathing, looking slightly forward and at the bottom of the pool.
● The level of the surface of the water should just cover the swimmer's ears.
● When breathing, the swimmer should have one goggle lens completely in the water and through the other goggle lens the swimmer should look across the surface of the pool.

Hips position
● The hips should be just under the surface of the water

Leg position

● The swimmer's leg should be close together, just under the surface of the water

Feet position
● The feet should be in a pointed (plantar flexion) position, which reduces drag and places them in the optimum position for maximum propulsion.

Body Rotation
● The swimmer should initiate a body rotation from their shoulders, trunk and hips, to facilitate a powerful arm pulling action and an effective breathing pattern.
● They should ensure that they don't over-rotate, as this could cause them to pull too deeply, which in turn could slow down their stroke rate and could contribute to an ineffective breathing pattern.

Chapter 2: The Body and Head Position

Introduction: The correct body and head position are extremely important in the development of a great competitive freestyle technique.

- It reduces drag and establishes the correct platform from which an effective arm stroke and leg kick can be performed.

The key components for an effective body and head position are:

- A horizontal and prone (on their front) body and leg position
- The head should be in a horizontal and prone position, in line with their body and legs, looking at the bottom of the pool, whilst swimming.
- The head should be positioned with one goggle lens in the water, and the other looking across the surface of the pool, whilst breathing.
- A smooth body rotation which, can help lengthen their stroke and should be initiated from the shoulders, trunk and hips.
- A strong and steady leg kick, which should raise the swimmer's legs to a horizontal position that reduces drag.
- Their feet should be in a pointed (plantar flexion) position, which reduces drag and places them in the optimum position for maximum propulsion.

2.1: Lateral kicking with a kickboard

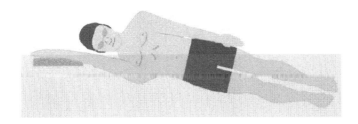

Purpose: This drill introduces the swimmer to lateral kicking, which can develop their body rotation to help lengthen their stroke.

How to perform this drill: The swimmer should start this drill from a push and glide from the wall at the end of the pool.

- The swimmer should rotate their body to their right-hand side (laterally).
- They should ensure that they hold the kickboard with a fully extended right arm, at the top edge while resting their right forearm on the kickboard.
- The swimmer should then start to freestyle leg kick on their right-hand side (laterally)
- They should place their left arm by their side.
- They should begin to perform a slow and steady freestyle leg kick (flutter kick) to keep the body as lateral as possible.
- The swimmer should complete this drill for one length/lap of the pool (25m)
- After a short rest interval, the swimmer should repeat this drill, but this time laterally kicking on their left-hand side.
- Younger and inexperienced swimmers may find it useful to use fins when first learning this drill.

2.2: Lateral kicking with a kickboard breathing on one goggle

Purpose: This drill further develops the lateral kicking technique, by introducing the correct head position while breathing during the freestyle stroke.

How to perform this drill: The swimmer should start this drill from a push and glide from the wall at the end of the pool.

• The swimmer should rotate their body on their right-hand side (laterally).

• The swimmer's head should be resting on the outstretched right arm.

• They should hold the edge of the kickboard with one hand

• They should have one goggle lens completely in the water and with the other goggle lens, they should look across the surface of the pool.

• The swimmer should complete this drill for one length/lap of the pool (25m) on their right-hand side.

• After a short rest interval, the swimmer should repeat this drill, but this time laterally kicking on their left-hand side.

• Younger and inexperienced swimmers may find it useful to use fins when first learning this drill.

2.3: Lateral kicking without a kickboard breathing on one goggle

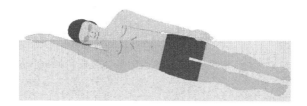

Purpose: This drill further develops the correct head position while breathing during the freestyle stroke.

How to perform this drill: The swimmer should start this drill from a push and glide from the wall at the end of the pool.

• The swimmer should rotate their body on their right-hand side (laterally).

• For this drill, the swimmer performs the lateral freestyle leg kicking drill without a kickboard.

• The swimmer's arm should be completely out-stretched in the catch position and that the swimmer's head should be resting upon it.

• They should have one goggle lens completely in the water and with the other goggle lens, they should look across the surface of the pool.

- The swimmer should complete this drill for one length/lap of the pool (25m) on their right-hand side.
- After a short rest interval, the swimmer should repeat this drill, but this time laterally kicking on their left-hand side.
- Younger and inexperienced swimmers may find it useful to use fins when first learning this drill.

2.4: Lateral kicking from side to side

Purpose: This drill further develops the correct head position while breathing during the freestyle stroke and introduces the swimmer to body rotation initiated from their shoulders, trunk and hips.

How to perform this drill: The swimmer should start this drill from a push and glide from the wall at the end of the pool.

- The swimmer should rotate their body on their right-hand side (laterally).
- They then start to perform five lateral freestyle leg kicks on their right-hand side, before rotating onto their left-hand side and repeating the five lateral freestyle leg kicks.
- Their arm should be completely out-stretched in the catch position and their head should be resting upon it.
- They should have one goggle lens completely in the water and with the other goggle lens, they should look across the surface of the pool.
- The swimmer should complete this drill for one length/lap of the pool (25m).
- Younger and inexperienced swimmers may find it useful to use fins when first learning this drill.

2.5: Lateral kicking 'hands in pockets'

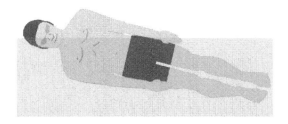

Purpose: This drill further develops the correct head position while breathing during the freestyle stroke, while further developing the swimmer's shoulder, trunk and hip rotation technique.

How to perform this drill: The swimmer should start this drill from a push and glide from the wall at the end of the pool.

● The swimmer should assume the lateral kicking position on their right-hand side.

● The swimmer should then place both of their arms by their sides, 'hands in pockets'.

● They should increase the intensity of their kick, on their side (laterally) steadily down the length of the pool.

● They should ensure that they perform a smooth and controlled body rotation initiated by their shoulders, trunk and hips.

● They should ensure that their body rotates completely from one side to the other, after every five lateral kicks.

● They should have one goggle lens completely in the water and with the other goggle lens, they should look across the surface of the pool.

● The swimmer should complete this drill for one length/lap of the pool (25m)

● Younger and inexperienced swimmers may find it useful to use fins when first learning this drill.

Chapter 3: Sculling

Introduction: Sculling is an often-overlooked key set of swimming skills.
● Efficient sculling skills can give the swimmer 'a feel for the water'.
● It can help them place their hands in the correct position, to help them to gain maximum propulsion during the completion of the arm stroke.
● Sculling can be great drills to introduce into a cool-down or recovery swim.

The sculling hand position
● The swimmer's fingers should be slightly apart, and the hands should be slightly cupped.

To obtain the correct hand position for sculling.
● The swimmer should place their hands on the cheeks of their face, ensuring that their fingers are very slightly apart.
● They should then remove their hands from their face, whilst keeping their fingers slightly apart.
● Their hands should now be in the optimum position for effective sculling.

3.1: Headfirst supine scull

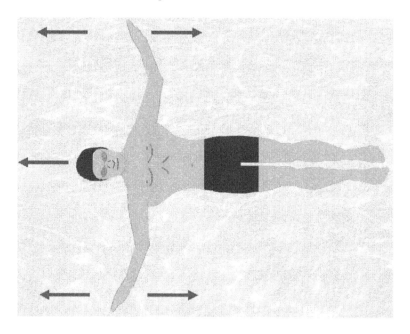

Purpose: This drill is a great introduction to a basic sculling technique.

How to perform this drill: The swimmer should start this drill from a push and glide from the wall at the end of the pool, in a horizontal supine (on their back) position.

● The swimmer's feet should be in a pointed plantar flexion position.

● The swimmer's arms should be outstretched, perpendicular to their body (90 degrees) with a slight bend at the elbow.

● The swimmer should perform a head-first scull.

● This should be achieved by performing a thumbs up scull on the downward scull, with their hands horizontal to the surface during the recovery scull.

● They should complete this drill for one length/lap of the pool (25m)

3.2: Feet first supine scull

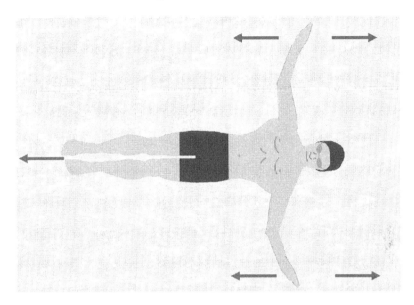

Purpose: This drill further develops the swimmer's basic sculling technique.

How to perform this drill: The swimmer should start this drill from a push and glide, feet first, from the wall at the end of the pool, in a horizontal supine (on their back) position.

● The swimmer's feet should be in a pointed plantar flexion position.

● The swimmer's arms should be outstretched, perpendicular to their body (90 degrees) with a slight bend at the elbow

● This should be achieved by performing a thumbs down scull on the upward scull, with their hands horizontal to the surface during the recovery scull.

● They should complete this drill for one length/lap of the pool (25m)

3.3: Headfirst prone scull

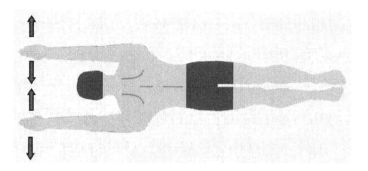

Purpose: This drill introduces the swimmer to a further basic scull, in a horizontal, face-down, prone position.

How to perform this drill: The swimmer should start this drill from a push and glide from the wall at the end of the pool, in a streamlined prone position (on their front) with their head in the water, lifting their head only to breathe.

● The swimmer's feet should be in a pointed plantar flexion position.

● The swimmer should move their outstretched arms to a position slightly wider than shoulder-width apart, with their palms down.

● The swimmer should perform this scull by moving their hands from side to side, with a thumbs down scull on the out-sweep and a thumbs up scull on the in-sweep.

● The swimmer should ensure they are performing a slight flutter (freestyle) kick.

● They should complete this drill for one length/lap of the pool (25m)

3.4: Doggy paddle

Purpose: An undervalued drill, doggy paddle is great for developing and maintaining the swimmer's sculling skills and feel for the water.

How to perform this drill: The swimmer should start this drill from a push and glide from the wall at the end of the pool, in a streamlined prone position (on their front), with their head out of the

water.
- The swimmer should proceed with a series of alternate arm sculls.
- They should extend their alternate arms fully into the catch position underwater.
- They should recover their arms with a sculling motion with their wrists up and their fingers pointing down to the bottom of the pool, in a straight line, back to their chest.
- They should perform a strong and steady flutter (freestyle) kick.
- Their feet should be in a pointed plantar flexion position.
- They should complete this drill for one length/lap of the pool (25m)

3.5: 'Seated' feet first scull

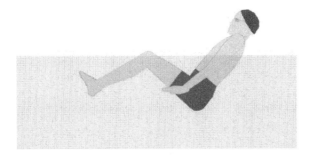

Purpose: This is an advanced sculling technique, which adds additional resistance.

How to perform this drill: The swimmer should start this drill at one end of the pool in a 'seated' (semi-recumbent), position.
- They should raise their knees and trunk into a semi-recumbent sitting position, with their body at approximately 45 degrees, although some swimmers may find it easier to sit in a more upright position.
- The swimmer's arms should be outstretched perpendicular to the swimmer's body (90 degrees) and bent at the elbow, the swimmer sculls feet first.
- This should be achieved by performing a thumbs down scull on the backward scull, with their hands horizontal to the surface during the recovery scull.
- They should complete this drill for one length/lap of the pool (25m)

3.6: Lateral scull

Purpose: This is an introductory lateral sculling drill.

● This can help to develop the correct sculling action required for an effective pull phase of the freestyle arm stroke.

How to perform this drill: The swimmer should start this drill from a push and glide from the wall at the end of the pool.

● The swimmer should rotate their body on their right-hand side (laterally), with their right arm fully outstretched, palm down in the catch position.

● The swimmer should then perform a lateral downward scull and should continue to scull down the body line until the arm is at right angles (45 degrees) to the swimmer's body.

● The swimmer should then recover their arm, by returning it to the catch position.

● They should have one goggle lens completely in the water and with the other goggle lens, they should look across the surface of the pool.

● They should complete this drill for one length/lap of the pool (25m)

● They should repeat this drill on the swimmer's left-hand side.

3.7: Lateral rotational sculls

Purpose: This is a further lateral sculling drill which introduces the swimmer to body rotation, which is initiated from their shoulders, trunk and hips.

• This can further help to develop the correct sculling action required for an effective pull phase of the freestyle arm stroke.

How to perform this drill: The swimmer should start this drill from a push and glide from the end wall at the end of the pool.

• The swimmer should rotate their body on their right-hand side (laterally), with their right arm fully outstretched, palm down in the catch position

• They should have one goggle lens completely in the water and with the other goggle lens, they should look across the surface of the pool.

• The swimmer should then perform a downward catch scull, then returns the arm to its original catch position.

• The swimmer should then rotate their body onto their left-hand side and repeat the drill.

• They should complete this drill for one length/lap of the pool (25m)

3.8: Lateral kicking - with a double lateral scull from side to side

Purpose: The last in a series of lateral sculling drills, which introduces the swimmer to a double lateral scull.

• This can further help to develop the correct sculling action required for an effective pull phase of the freestyle arm stroke.

How to perform this drill: The swimmer should start this drill from a push and glide from the end wall at the end of the pool.

• The swimmer should rotate their body on their right-hand side (laterally), with their right arm fully outstretched, palm down in the catch position.

• They should have one goggle lens completely in the water and with the other goggle lens, they should look across the surface of the pool.

• The swimmer should then perform two downward catch sculls, then returns their arm to its original catch position.

• The swimmer should then rotate their body onto their left-hand side and repeat the drill.

FREESTYLE Competitive Swimming Drills

- They should complete this drill for one length/lap of the pool (25m)

Chapter 4: Breathing Techniques

Introduction: A common freestyle breathing fault, is that swimmers often hold their breath while their face is in the water.

● They then attempt to exhale and inhale quickly while their face is out of the water.

● This results in the swimmer being in a non-streamlined breathing position for longer, which increases drag and can slow the swimmer down.

● It is also an ineffective method at supplying the oxygen that is required to the swimmer's muscles and organs during training and competition.

Trickle breathing

● Trickle breathing is a breathing technique that can help the swimmer develop a faster, better streamlined and efficient breathing technique.

● It requires the swimmer to take a large quick breath, then to slowly exhale in the water via their nose or their mouth

● This technique can also enable the swimmer to stay longer underwater while performing underwater dolphin kicking during their starts and turns.

4.1: Trickle breathing development poolside

Purpose: This drill introduces the swimmer to trickle breathing, which can aid the development of an effective breathing pattern.

How to perform this drill: This drill should be practised on the poolside/deck in a safe place away from the pool's edge.

● The swimmer should start this drill by taking a large quick breath, which fills their lungs.

● They should then put up their hand.

● The swimmer should then breathe out very slowly, via their nose or mouth ('trickle breathe') until they have no breath left.

● When they are out of breath, they should quickly lower their hand, then resume normal breathing.

● The coach should time and record this drill.

● This should demonstrate to the swimmer that by adopting trickle breathing, the swimmer has enough time to perform either underwater dolphin kicking or their preferred freestyle breathing pattern efficiently.

4.2: Trickle breathing development – pool

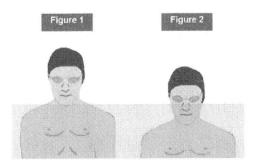

Figure 1   Figure 2

Purpose: This drill introduces the swimmer to trickle breathing in the water.

How to perform this drill: The swimmer should start this drill by standing up straight, waist-deep in the water.

• They should then bend their knees, lowering themselves into the water until their chin is touching the surface (Figure 1).

• They should then take a large quick breath, which fills their lungs.

• Then the swimmer should lower themselves still further into the water until it has covered both their nose and mouth, just below the rim of their goggles (Figure 2).

• They should start to breathe out in the water very slowly, via their nose or mouth ('trickle breathe') until they have no breath left.

• When they are out of breath, the swimmer should then raise themselves back to the starting position.

• The swimmer should repeat this drill six times.

4.3: Trickle breathing development - pool 2

Purpose: This is a great freestyle breathing drill, for further introducing the swimmer to the trickle breathing technique.

How to perform this drill: The swimmer should enter the pool, holding a kickboard and should stand in the water up to their waist.

● They should hold the kickboard, with both hands, grasping the outer edges.

● They should then take a large quick breath, which fills their lungs.

● Then they should bend at the hips until their face is in the water and they are looking down at the bottom of the pool.

● They should then exhale in the water.

● When they have finished exhaling, they should turn their head to the side, still with their head in the water, until their mouth is just above the surface and then they inhale.

● After they have finished inhaling, they should then turn their head downward into the original exhaling position.

● Once the swimmer has mastered this exercise, they should repeat this exercise a further six times.

● Breathing three times on their right-hand side and three times on their left-hand side.

● When breathing, they should have one goggle lens completely in the water and with the other goggle lens, they should look across the surface of the pool.

4.4: Trickle breathing pattern development

Purpose: This is a further trickle breathing drill to help further develop an effective breathing pattern.

How to perform this drill: The swimmer should start this drill from a push & glide from the wall at the end of the pool.

- They should proceed by performing a slow and smooth, full freestyle stroke.
- They should ensure that when breathing, they take a large quick breath, that fills their lungs.
- When breathing, they should have one goggle lens completely in the water and with the other goggle lens, they should look across the surface of the pool.
- They should then slowly let out their breath in the water via their nose or their mouth (trickle breathe), as they swim.
- They should count how many strokes they can comfortably swim before they need to take a breath.
- They should complete this drill for one length/lap of the pool (25m).
- Younger and inexperienced swimmers may find it useful to use fins when first learning this drill.

4.5: Bilateral breathing

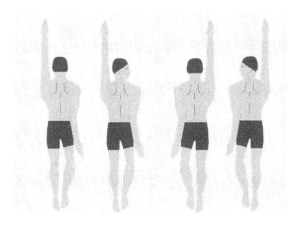

The key components for an effective bilateral breathing technique are:
- The body should be in a horizontal prone (on their front) position.
- The head should be in a horizontal and prone position, in line with their body and legs, looking at the bottom of the pool, whilst swimming.
- A low head position, with one goggle lens in the water, and the other looking across the surface of the pool, whilst breathing.
- A smooth and controlled rotation of the body, initiated from the

shoulders, trunk and hips.

● A strong and steady freestyle leg kick.

Purpose: Bilateral breathing is breathing to both sides while swimming freestyle.

● Bilateral breathing establishes a regular breathing pattern, which is more effective at supplying oxygen to the muscles and organs.

● It also balances the stroke, enabling the swimmer to take a longer stroke on their non-breathing side.

How to perform this drill: Starting from a push & glide, from the end of the pool, the swimmer should perform an easy and smooth freestyle stroke.

● They should commence breathing bilaterally.

● Breathing every three strokes on one side then breathing every three strokes on the other side.

● When breathing, they should have one goggle lens completely in the water and with the other goggle lens, they should look across the surface of the pool.

● The swimmer should ensure that they are performing 'trickle breathing' while they are performing this drill.

● They should complete this drill for one length/lap of the pool (25m).

● Younger and inexperienced swimmers may find it useful to use fins when first learning this drill.

4.6: Bilateral breathing development

Purpose: This drill can help to further develop an effective bilateral breathing pattern.

How to perform this drill: The swimmer should start this drill from a push & glide, from the end of the pool.

- They should perform an easy and smooth freestyle stroke.
- The swimmer should perform a bilateral breathing pattern breathing every five strokes, without any deterioration of their stroke technique.
- When breathing, they should have one goggle lens completely in the water and with the other goggle lens, they should look across the surface of the pool.
- The swimmer should ensure that they are performing 'trickle breathing' while they are performing this drill.
- Once the swimmer has mastered this drill, this can be extended to every seven strokes, eventually working up to every nine strokes.
- They should complete this drill for one length/lap of the pool (25m).
- Younger and inexperienced swimmers may find it useful to use fins when first learning this drill.

Variation: Once mastered, the swimmer may be introduced to mixed bilateral breathing patterns. For example, bilateral breathing alternate lengths/laps for every three and every five strokes.

4.7: Stretch on the breath

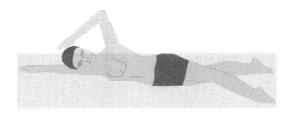

Purpose: This drill helps to develop the swimmer's stroke length, while bilaterally breathing.

How to perform this drill: The swimmer should start this drill from a push & glide, from the end of the pool.

- They should perform an easy and smooth freestyle stroke.
- The swimmer should perform a bilateral breathing pattern, breathing every three strokes.
- The swimmer should fully extend their leading arm, to the catch position when breathing.
- They should hold this extended position for three leg kicks, before recommencing with an easy and smooth freestyle stroke.
- When breathing, they should have one goggle lens completely in the water and with the other goggle lens, they should look across the surface of the pool.

- The swimmer should ensure that they are performing 'trickle breathing' while they are performing this drill.
- They should complete this drill for one length/lap of the pool (25m).
- Younger and inexperienced swimmers may find it useful to use fins when first learning this drill.

4.8: Trailing fingers

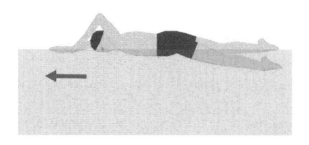

Purpose: This is an excellent drill for developing a high elbow action, which facilitates maximum stroke length while breathing bilaterally.

How to perform this drill: The swimmer should start this drill from a push & glide, from the end of the pool.

- They should perform an easy and smooth freestyle stroke.
- The swimmer should perform a bilateral breathing pattern, breathing every three strokes.
- As the arm exits the water during the recovery phase, the swimmer should keep their elbow as high as possible, while trailing their fingertips across the surface of the pool back to the extended catch position.
- When breathing, they should have one goggle lens completely in the water and with the other goggle lens, they should look across the surface of the pool.
- The swimmer should ensure that they are performing 'trickle breathing' while they are performing this drill.
- They should complete this drill for one length/lap of the pool (25m).
- Younger and inexperienced swimmers may find it useful to use fins when first learning this drill.

4.9: Monkey drill

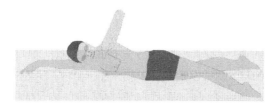

Purpose: This is another excellent drill for developing a high elbow action, which facilitates maximum stroke length while breathing bilaterally.

How to perform this drill: The swimmer should start this drill from a push & glide, from the end of the pool.

• They should perform an easy and smooth freestyle stroke.

• The swimmer should perform a bilateral breathing pattern, breathing every three strokes.

• As the arm exits the water into the recovery phase, the swimmer should keep their elbow as high as possible and touch their armpit with their fingers.

• The swimmer completes the stroke by, trailing their fingertips across the surface of the pool back to the extended catch position.

• When breathing, they should have one goggle lens completely in the water and with the other goggle lens, they should look across the surface of the pool.

• The swimmer should ensure that they are performing 'trickle breathing' while they are performing this drill.

• They should complete this drill for one length/lap of the pool (25m).

• Younger and inexperienced swimmers may find it useful to use fins when first learning this drill.

4.10: Bilateral breathing with hesitation

Purpose: This is another excellent drill for developing a high elbow action, which facilitates maximum stroke length while breathing bilaterally.

How to perform this drill: The swimmer should start this drill from a push & glide, from the end of the pool.

● They should perform an easy and smooth freestyle stroke.

● The swimmer should perform a bilateral breathing pattern breathing every three strokes.

● As their hand comes out of the water for the recovery phase, the swimmer should rest their hand on their cheek for three leg kicks.

● The swimmer completes the stroke by, trailing their fingertips across the surface of the pool back to the extended catch position.

● When breathing, they should have one goggle lens completely in the water and with the other goggle lens, they should look across the surface of the pool.

● The swimmer should ensure that they are performing 'trickle breathing' while they are performing this drill.

● They should complete this drill for one length/lap of the pool (25m)

● Younger and inexperienced swimmers may find it useful to use fins when first learning this drill.

Chapter 5: The Leg Kick

Introduction: Kicking is an important and sometimes undervalued key swimming skill, and as such should be constantly and consistently practised.
● The leg kick can provide secondary propulsion to the freestyle stroke.
● An effective leg kick can raise the swimmer's legs to a horizontal position, thus reducing drag.
● As the leg muscles are amongst the largest in the body, having a trained, effective leg kick minimises energy and oxygen consumption, whilst maximising propulsion.

The key components for an effective leg kick are:
● Kicking should be initiated from their thighs (quads), hamstrings and buttocks (glutes), using the largest muscles in the body to drive propulsion.
● There should be minimal knee bend, one the most common faults while freestyle leg kicking.
● Kicking with a bent knee increases drag and uses the relatively smaller calf muscles.
● Their feet should be in a pointed (plantar flexion) position.

5.1: Vertical kicking

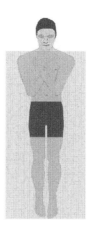

Purpose: Vertical freestyle kicking is a great introductory kicking drill which can also help to improve the swimmer's ankle flexibility.

How to perform this drill: The swimmer should start this drill in a vertical position, in water deep enough so they cannot touch the bottom.

- They should perform a slow and steady freestyle leg (flutter) kick.
- They should fold their arms across their chest.
- They should ensure that they keep their chin level on the surface.
- Younger and inexperienced swimmers may find it useful to use fins or a kickboard when first learning this drill.

Variations: The swimmer can increase the intensity of the leg kick required, in three stages

- Level1: By raising their shoulders out of the water.
- Level 2: By raising their hands and forearms out of the water.
- Level 3: By raising their arms out of the water, in a streamlined position.

5.2: Kicking with a kickboard

Purpose: This is a classic drill for helping to develop an effective freestyle (flutter) leg kick by isolating the swimmer's legs, with the use of a kickboard.

• Kickboards are an essential part of any competitive swimmer's kit.

How to perform this drill: The swimmer should start this drill from a streamlined push and glide from the end of the pool, whilst holding the kickboard with fully extended arms.

• They should commence a steady freestyle leg kick in a horizontal and prone position while keeping their head out of the water.

• The swimmer should ensure that they are holding the kickboard with fully extended arms at its top edge and they are resting their forearms on the kickboard.

• The swimmer should then perform a slow, steady and shallow freestyle leg kick.

• They should focus on kicking from their thighs (quads), hamstrings and buttocks (glutes).

• The swimmer should focus on eliminating any knee bend.

• They should ensure that their feet are in a pointed (plantar flexion) position.

• They should complete this drill for one length/lap of the pool (25m).

• Younger and inexperienced swimmers may find it useful to use fins when first learning this drill.

5.3: Kicking builds

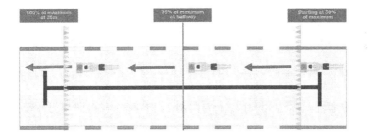

Purpose: An introductory drill to kicking speed play, which can help strengthen and develop the swimmer's freestyle leg kick.

How to perform this drill: The swimmer should start this drill from a streamlined push and glide from the end of the pool, whilst holding a kickboard with fully extended arms.

• They should commence performing a steady freestyle leg kick in a horizontal and prone position while keeping their head out of the water.

• The swimmer should start kicking at approximately 50% of their maximum leg kick speed.

- They should gradually increase the speed of their kick over one length.
- The swimmer should be at approximately 75% of their maximum leg kick speed at half-way.
- Without deterioration of their kicking technique, the swimmer should be close to reaching their maximum leg kick speed as they approach the finish of the length/lap.
- They should focus on kicking from their thighs (quads), hamstrings and buttocks (glutes).
- The swimmer should also focus on eliminating any knee bend.
- They should ensure that their feet are in a pointed (plantar flexion) position.
- Younger and inexperienced swimmers may find it useful to use fins when first learning this drill.

5.4: Kicking speed play

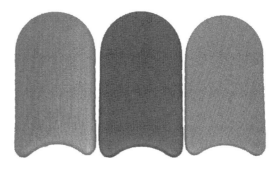

Purpose: This is a speed play kicking drill which can help strengthen and develop the swimmer's freestyle leg kick.

How to perform this drill: The swimmer should start this drill from a streamlined push and glide from the end of the pool, whilst holding a kickboard with fully extended arms.

- They should be in a horizontal and prone position while keeping their head out of the water.
- The swimmer should then perform ten slow leg kicks, and then they should perform ten fast leg kicks (10/10), initially over 50m.
- They should focus on kicking from their thighs (quads), hamstrings and buttocks (glutes).
- The swimmer should also focus on eliminating any knee bend.
- They should ensure that their feet are in a pointed (plantar flexion) position.

● Younger and inexperienced swimmers may find it useful to use fins or a kickboard when first learning this drill.

Variation: Once mastered this drill can be made more difficult by progressively reducing the number of slow and fast leg kicks.

● For example, seven fast leg kicks, then seven slow leg kicks (7/7)

5.5: Kicking speed play on the whistle

Purpose: This is another speed play drill which can help further develop and maintain a strong freestyle leg kick.

How to perform this drill: The swimmer should start this drill from a streamlined push and glide from the end of the pool, whilst holding the kickboard with fully extended arms.

● They should commence a slow and steady freestyle leg kick in a horizontal and prone position while keeping their head out of the water.

● The coach should then blow a whistle which is the signal for the swimmer to perform a fast freestyle leg kick at sprint speed until the coach blows the whistle again and the swimmer should then return to a slow and steady kick.

● These bouts of random fast and slow kicking should be repeated, initially over 50m/100m.

● The intensity of this set should be gradually increased, by a combination of longer fast intervals, shorter rests or by slowly increasing the distance.

● Younger and inexperienced swimmers may find it useful to use fins when first learning this drill.

5.6: Resistance kicking with a kickboard

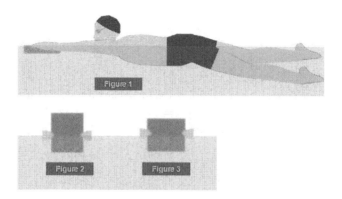

Purpose: This is another excellent drill for helping to develop a strong freestyle leg kick by adding additional resistance.

How to perform this drill: The swimmer should start this drill from a streamlined push and glide from the end of the pool, whilst holding the kickboard with fully extended arms.

● They should commence a slow and steady freestyle leg kick in a horizontal and prone position while keeping their head out of the water.

● However, instead of holding the kickboard horizontal on the surface at the top edge of the kickboard (figure 1), the swimmer should hold the kickboard vertically upright, so that half the kickboard is under the surface (figure 2).

● For increased resistance, the swimmer should hold the kickboard horizontally upright, so again half the kickboard is under the surface (figure 3).

● They should complete this drill for one length/lap of the pool (25m).

5.7: Partner kicking with kickboards

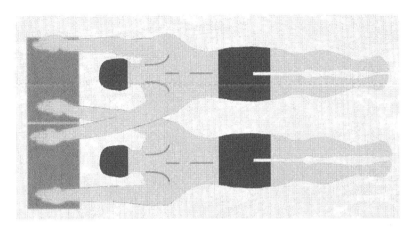

Purpose: This is another excellent drill to further help develop a strong freestyle leg kick.

How to perform this drill: The swimmer should pick a kicking partner.

● This drill works better if the swimmers are roughly of the same size and ability.

● With both swimmers in the water, side by side, each should be holding a kickboard.

● The swimmer on the left should place their left hand on their kickboard and should place their right hand on their partner's kickboard.

● The swimmer on the right should place their right hand on their kickboard and should place their left hand on their partner's kickboard.

● From a push & glide at the end of the pool, both swimmers should perform a freestyle flutter kick for one length/lap of the pool (25m).

5.8: Trio kicking with kickboards

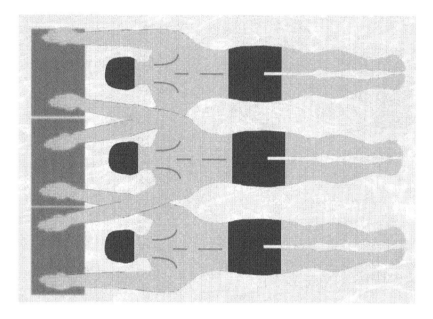

Purpose: This is another excellent drill to further help develop a strong freestyle leg kick.

freestyle leg kick, which also adds a bit of fun.

How to perform this drill: For this drill, the swimmers should work in threes.

● This drill works better if the swimmers are roughly of the same size and ability.

● With each swimmer in the water, side by side, each should be holding a kickboard.

● The swimmer on the left should place their left hand on their kickboard and should place their right hand on the swimmer in the middle's kickboard.

● The swimmer on the right should place their right hand on their kickboard and should place their left hand on the swimmer in the middle's kickboard.

● The swimmer in the middle should place their left arm on the swimmer on the left's kickboard and should place their right arm on the swimmer on the right's kickboard.

● From a push & glide at the end of the pool, both swimmers should perform a freestyle flutter kick for one length/lap of the pool (25m).

Chapter 6: The Arm Stroke

Introduction:

The main propulsive force during the freestyle stroke comes from the arm pull.

● This is aided by a smooth and controlled body rotation, which is initiated from their shoulders, trunk and hips.

● As they perform the freestyle stroke, the swimmer should focus on pushing the water backwards towards their feet, to generate propulsion.

● The swimmer should also ensure that they pull down the centre of their body, without crossing their hands over to the other side of their body.

The key components for an effective arm pull

Hand and arm entry
- The swimmer's hand should enter the water in front of their head midway between their shoulder and their head.
- They should tilt their hand at an approximate forty-five degrees

angle.

● This should ensure that their thumb, index and middle fingers enter the water first.

● The swimmer should fully extend their arm approximately 4 inches (10 cm) under the surface.

The down-sweep
● The swimmer should scull outwards, just past level with their shoulder to catch the water.

● The swimmer should then bend their wrist so that their fingertips are pointing towards the bottom of the pool, while bending their elbow, but still keeping it high in the water.

● The swimmer should then move their hand and arm in a downward direction while keeping their fingertips pointing towards the bottom of the pool.

● As the swimmer performs their down-sweep they should begin to bend their elbow, and their hand should start to accelerate.

The in-sweep
● As the swimmer completes their down-sweep of their hand and arm, the swimmer should start the in-sweep, towards the centre line of their body by continuing to increase their elbow flexion until it reaches approximately ninety degrees.

The up-sweep
● As the swimmer completes the in-sweep, they should start their up-sweep by adjusting the pitch of their hand so that they once more have their fingertips pointing towards the bottom of the pool.

● The swimmer should ensure that they fully complete their stroke by continuing to push the water backwards past their hip until their arm is fully extended.

● Once their arm is fully extended, they should rotate their hand, so their palm brushes their thigh in preparation for the recovery.

Recovery
● The recovery is led by the elbow.

● The swimmer should bend their elbow as it leaves the water, close to the swimmer's head.

● This should be followed by their hand, little finger first.

● The swimmer's elbow should remain bent and remains higher than their arm throughout the recovery.

● The arm and hand should start to move forward to begin their entry.

6.1: Single arm pulling with a kickboard

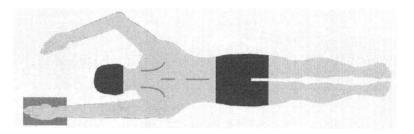

Introduction: Single-arm freestyle pulling is an excellent way of isolating and developing the freestyle arm stroke.
● It can also help to develop and maintain a strong freestyle leg kick.

Purpose: This is an introductory drill to single-arm pulling.

How to perform this drill: The swimmer should start this drill from a push and glide from the end of the pool, in a horizontal and prone streamlined position.
● They should be holding a kickboard in their left hand with a fully extended left arm.
● The swimmer should then perform a series of drill pace, long freestyle right arm pulls.
● They should ensure that they have a high elbow on the recovery phase of the arm pull, to assist maximum stroke length.
● Their head should be in a horizontal and prone position, in line with their body and legs, looking at the bottom of the pool, whilst pulling.
● When breathing, they should have one goggle lens completely in the water and with the other goggle lens, they should look across the surface of the pool.
● They should maintain a strong and steady leg kick.
● Their feet should be in a pointed (plantar flexion) position.
● They should complete this drill for one length/lap of the pool (25m)
● Once mastered the swimmer should repeat this drill by performing a series of left-arm pulls.

6.2: Single arm pulling with extended arm

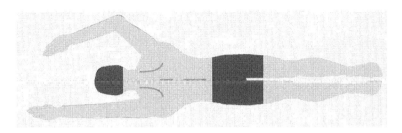

Purpose: This drill introduces the swimmer to single-arm pulling without a kickboard.

How to perform this drill: The swimmer should start this drill from a push and glide from the end of the pool in a horizontal and prone streamlined position.

● They should have a fully extended left arm.

● The swimmer should then perform a series of drill pace, long freestyle right arm pulls.

● They should ensure that they have a high elbow on the recovery phase of the arm pull, to assist maximum stroke length.

● Their head should be in a horizontal and prone position, in line with their body and legs, looking at the bottom of the pool, whilst pulling.

● When breathing, they should have one goggle lens completely in the water and with the other goggle lens, they should look across the surface of the pool.

● They should maintain a strong and steady leg kick.

● Their feet should be in a pointed (plantar flexion) position.

● They should complete this drill for one length/lap of the pool (25m)

● Once mastered the swimmer should repeat this drill by performing a series of left-arm pulls.

6.3: Single arm pulling hand in pocket

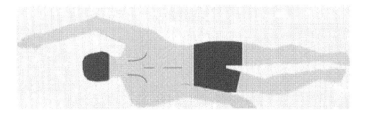

Purpose: A further single-arm development drill without a kickboard, where the swimmer places their non-pulling arm by their side.

How to perform this drill: The swimmer should start this drill from a push and glide from the end of the pool in a horizontal and prone streamlined position.

● Their left arm should be down by their side

● The swimmer should then perform a series of drill pace, long freestyle right arm pulls.

● They should ensure that they have a high elbow on the recovery phase of the arm pull, to assist maximum stroke length.

● Their head should be in a horizontal and prone position, in line with their body and legs, looking at the bottom of the pool, whilst pulling.

● When breathing, they should have one goggle lens completely in the water and with the other goggle lens, they should look across the surface of the pool.

● They should maintain a strong and steady leg kick.

● Their feet should be in a pointed (plantar flexion) position.

● They should complete this drill for one length/lap of the pool (25m)

● Once mastered the swimmer should repeat this drill by performing a series of left-arm pulls.

6.4: Single arm pulling with alternate arms

Purpose: A further single-arm development drill using both arms alternately.

How to perform this drill: The swimmer should start this drill from a push and glide from the end of the pool in a horizontal and prone streamlined position.

● They should have a fully extended left arm.

● The swimmer should proceed to perform three drill pace, long freestyle right arm pulls.

● They should then switch arm positions, by fully extending right arm.

● They should then perform three drill pace, long freestyle left arm pulls.

● They should ensure that they have a high elbow on the recovery phase of the arm pull, to assist maximum stroke length.

• Their head should be in a horizontal and prone position, in line with their body and legs, looking at the bottom of the pool, whilst pulling.

• When breathing, they should have one goggle lens completely in the water and with the other goggle lens, they should look across the surface of the pool.

• They should maintain a strong and steady leg kick.

• Their feet should be in a pointed (plantar flexion) position.

• They should complete this drill for one length/lap of the pool (25m)

6.5: Catch up drill

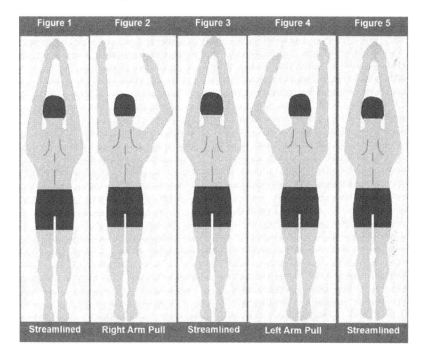

Purpose: This is a classic multi-functional freestyle drill which can help to develop and maintain the swimmer's stroke technique.

• This drill not only develops the freestyle arm stroke but also, their kicking and breathing techniques.

How to perform this drill: The swimmer should start this drill in the streamline position (figure1)

• The swimmer should ensure that their left arm remains fully extended into the catch position, whilst their right arm performs a full freestyle stroke (figure 2), until it 'catches up' with the fully extended left arm, back into a streamlined position. (figure 3)

● The left arm should now perform a full freestyle stroke (figure 4) until it 'catches up' with the right arm back into a streamlined position (figure 5).

● Their head should be in a horizontal and prone position, in line with their body and legs, looking at the bottom of the pool, whilst pulling.

● When breathing, they should have one goggle lens completely in the water and with the other goggle lens, they should look across the surface of the pool.

● They should maintain a strong and steady leg kick.

● Their feet should be in a pointed (plantar flexion) position.

● They should complete this drill for one length/lap of the pool (25m)

Variation: Some swimmers try to rush this drill and don't always wait for one arm to 'catch-up' with the other.

● In this case, a variation on this drill should be introduced, whereby once one hand has caught up with the other, the swimmer completes three leg kicks in a streamlined position before they can proceed with the next arm pull.

6.6: Zipper drill

Purpose: This is another classic freestyle drill, which helps to develop a high elbow recovery.

How to perform this drill: The swimmer should start this drill from a push and glide from the end of the pool in a horizontal and prone streamlined position, performing a full freestyle stroke at drill pace.

● On the recovery phase of each stroke, the swimmer should drag their thumb up and along the side of their body from their thigh to their armpit.

● Mimicking the actions of closing a zipper.

● Their head should be in a horizontal and prone position, in line with their body and legs, looking at the bottom of the pool, whilst pulling.

● When breathing, they should have one goggle lens completely in the water and with the other goggle lens, they should look across the surface of the pool.

● They should maintain a strong and steady leg kick.

- Their feet should be in a pointed (plantar flexion) position.
- They should complete this drill for one length/lap of the pool (25m).

6.7: Kickboard pull

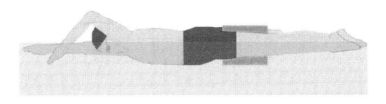

Purpose: This is an excellent pulling drill for developing and maintaining the stroke's exit phase, as well as stroke length.

How to perform this drill: The swimmer should start this drill from a push and glide from the end of the pool in a horizontal and prone streamlined position, performing a full freestyle stroke at drill pace, with a kickboard placed between their thighs.

- At the end of the exit phase of each stroke, the swimmer should touch the kickboard with the palm of their hand.
- Their head should be in a horizontal and prone position, in line with their body and legs, looking at the bottom of the pool, whilst pulling.
- When breathing, they should have one goggle lens completely in the water and with the other goggle lens, they should look across the surface of the pool.
- Their feet should be in a pointed (plantar flexion) position.
- They should complete this drill for one length/lap of the pool (25m)

Pull buoy pulling drills

Introduction: The use of a pull buoy is an excellent way of isolating the swimmer's arms to help develop and maintain their upper body strength.
- A pull buoy is an essential part of any competitive swimmer's kit.

The key components for an effective arm pull are:
- Pulling should be performed with a high elbow on the recovery phase, to assist maximum stroke length.
- Although pull buoys can restrict the body's rotation, the swimmer should focus on achieving maximum stroke length.
- Their head should be in a horizontal and prone position, in line with their body and legs, looking at the bottom of the pool, whilst pulling.
- When breathing, they should have one goggle lens completely in the water and with the other goggle lens, they should look across the surface of the pool.
- Their feet should be in a pointed (plantar flexion) position.

6.8: Pulling pyramid

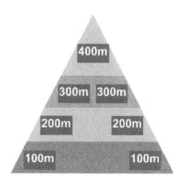

Purpose: This is a classic arm pulling drill, a great way of developing an effective arm stroke.

How to perform this drill: The swimmer should start this drill from a push and glide from the end of the pool in a horizontal and prone streamlined position, with a pull buoy between their thighs.
- They should swim a given distance while performing a freestyle arm stroke only.
- This drill can be conducted over repeat sets of 100m/200m or, as I prefer, conducting a 'pyramid' in 100m steps.
- For example, 100m, 200m, 300m, 400m, 300m, 200m, 100m (steps of 50m for younger swimmers).
- Emphasis should be on a great technique, with high elbows on

the recovery phase and a long, strong and controlled pulling action.
• Although pull buoys can restrict the body's rotation, the swimmer should focus on achieving maximum stroke length.
• Their head should be in a horizontal and prone position, in line with their body and legs, looking at the bottom of the pool, whilst pulling.
• When breathing, they should have one goggle lens completely in the water and with the other goggle lens, they should look across the surface of the pool.
• Their feet should be in a pointed (plantar flexion) position.

6.9: Pulling builds

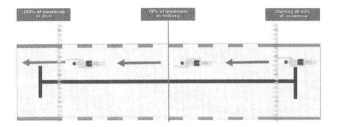

Purpose: An introductory pulling speed play drill which can help strengthen and develop the freestyle arm pull.
How to perform this drill: The swimmer should start this drill from a push and glide from the end of the pool in a horizontal and prone streamlined position, with a pull buoy between their thighs.
• They should proceed to perform a freestyle arm stroke only.
• The swimmer should start pulling at approximately 50% of their maximum speed.
• The swimmer should then slowly increase the speed of their pull over the distance of one length/lap (25m).
• The swimmer should at approximately 75% of their maximum speed at halfway and be close to reaching maximum arm speed as they approach the finish of the length/lap.
• Emphasis should be on a great technique, with high elbows on the recovery phase and a long, strong and controlled pulling action.
• Although pull buoys can restrict the body's rotation, the swimmer should focus on achieving maximum stroke length.
• Their head should be in a horizontal and prone position, in line with their body and legs, looking at the bottom of the pool, whilst pulling.
• When breathing, they should have one goggle lens completely in

the water and with the other goggle lens, they should look across the surface of the pool.

● Their feet should be in a pointed (plantar flexion) position.

6.10: Pulling with hand paddles

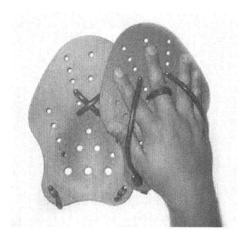

Purpose: This arm pulling drill introduces the swimmer to hand paddles.

● Hand paddles are an excellent piece of kit for adding resistance and intensity to any pulling drill.

● They come in many different varieties.

● Please ensure the swimmer has the correct type of hand paddles for their size and ability.

How to perform this drill: The swimmer should start this drill from a push and glide from the end of the pool in a horizontal and prone streamlined position, wearing their hand paddles.

● This drill can be conducted over repeat sets of 100m/200m or, as I prefer, conducting a 'pyramid' in 100m steps.

● For example, 100m, 200m, 300m, 400m, 300m, 200m, 100m (steps of 50m for younger swimmers).

● Emphasis should be on a great technique, with high elbows on the recovery phase and a long, strong and controlled pulling action.

● Their head should be in a horizontal and prone position, in line with their body and legs, looking at the bottom of the pool, whilst pulling.

● When breathing, they should have one goggle lens completely in the water and with the other goggle lens, they should look across the surface of the pool.

● Their feet should be in a pointed (plantar flexion) position.

• This drill can be performed with or without a pull buoy.

6.11: Pulling with fists

Purpose: This drill introduces the swimmer to pulling with clenched fists.

• This adds extra resistance to the arm pull.

• It necessitates the swimmer pulling longer and harder and using their forearms as means of propulsion.

• Often once a swimmer has completed this drill with fists when they go back to normal pulling with unclenched fists, most swimmers develop a better feel for the water and therefore some swimmers pull more effectively.

How to perform this drill: The swimmer should start this drill from a push and glide from the end of the pool in a horizontal and prone streamlined position, with clenched fists.

• This drill can be conducted over repeat sets of 100m/200m or, as I prefer, conducting a 'pyramid' in 100m steps.

• For example, 100m, 200m, 300m, 400m, 300m, 200m, 100m (steps of 50m for younger swimmers).

• Emphasis should be on a great technique, with high elbows on the recovery phase and a long, strong and controlled pulling action.

• Their head should be in a horizontal and prone position, in line with their body and legs, looking at the bottom of the pool, whilst pulling.

• When breathing, they should have one goggle lens completely in the water and with the other goggle lens, they should look across the surface of the pool.

• Their feet should be in a pointed (plantar flexion) position.

• This drill can be performed with or without a pull buoy.

6.12: Pulling with fists and open hands

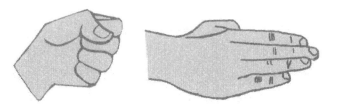

Purpose: This arm pulling drill can help develop the swimmer's 'feel for the water' by the introduction of alternate clenched fists and open hands swimming.

How to perform this drill: The swimmer should start this drill from a push and glide from the end of the pool in a horizontal and prone streamlined position, with clenched fists.

• The swimmer should proceed to swim six arm strokes with clenched fists and six strokes with normal open hands.

• Emphasis should be on a great technique, with high elbows on the recovery phase and a long, strong and controlled pulling action.

• Their head should be in a horizontal and prone position, in line with their body and legs, looking at the bottom of the pool, whilst pulling.

• When breathing, they should have one goggle lens completely in the water and with the other goggle lens, they should look across the surface of the pool.

• Their feet should be in a pointed (plantar flexion) position.

• They should complete this drill for one length/lap of the pool (25m)

• This drill can be performed with or without a pull buoy.

6.13: Pulling with tennis balls

Purpose: This drill can add extra intensity to a swimmer's arm pulls, by the introduction of swimming while holding two tennis balls.

• The extra buoyancy generated by the tennis balls, requires the swimmer to focus on an effective pulling action.

How to perform this drill: The swimmer should start this drill from a push and glide from the end of the pool in a horizontal and prone streamlined position, holding a tennis ball in each hand.

● Emphasis should be on a great technique, with high elbows on the recovery phase and a long, strong and controlled pulling action.

● Their head should be in a horizontal and prone position, in line with their body and legs, looking at the bottom of the pool, whilst pulling.

● When breathing, they should have one goggle lens completely in the water and with the other goggle lens, they should look across the surface of the pool.

● Their feet should be in a pointed (plantar flexion) position.

● They should complete this drill for one length/lap of the pool (25m)

● This drill can be performed with or without a pull buoy.

6.14: Pulling with streamlined legs

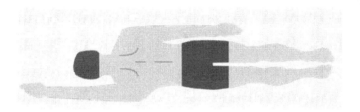

Purpose: This arm pulling drill, without a pull buoy combines arm pulling and core strength development.

How to perform this drill: The swimmer should start this drill from a push & glide at the end of the pool, in a streamlined horizontal and prone position (on their front).

● They should focus on keeping their legs motionless and in a streamlined position throughout this drill, without allowing their legs to drop.

● The swimmer should engage their core while performing this drill*.

● Emphasis should be on a great technique, with high elbows on the recovery phase and a long, strong and controlled pulling action.

● Their head should be in a horizontal and prone position, in line with their body and legs, looking at the bottom of the pool, whilst pulling.

● When breathing, they should have one goggle lens completely in the water and with the other goggle lens, they should look across the surface of the pool.

● Their feet should be in a pointed (plantar flexion) position.

● They should complete this drill for one length/lap of the pool (25m)
Variation: Some coaches prefer their swimmers to perform this drill using an ankle strap/band.
● These can place over their ankles to help eliminate kicking when pulling.

6.15: Pulling with crossed legs

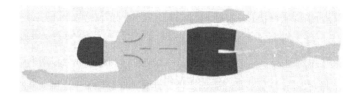

Purpose: A further arm pulling drill, without a pull buoy which combines arm pulling and core strength development.
How to perform this drill: The swimmer should start this drill from a push & glide at the end of the pool, in a streamlined horizontal and prone position (on their front), while keeping their legs crossed.
● They should focus on keeping their legs motionless and in a streamlined position, throughout this drill, without allowing their legs to drop.
● The swimmer should engage their core while performing this drill*.
● Emphasis should be on a great technique, with high elbows on the recovery phase and a long, strong and controlled pulling action.
● Their head should be in a horizontal and prone position, in line with their body and legs, looking at the bottom of the pool, whilst pulling.
● When breathing, they should have one goggle lens completely in the water and with the other goggle lens, they should look across the surface of the pool.
● Their feet should be in a pointed (plantar flexion) position.
● They should complete this drill for one length/lap of the pool (25m)

*How to engage your core
Engaging your core muscles ensures they are correctly aligned, to help support and perform certain swimming drills and skills effectively.
● To engage their core, the swimmer should continue to breathe normally.
● They should then tighten/contract their stomach muscles while drawing their navel towards their spine.

Core strength development

To effectively engage their core, the swimmer should develop their core strength.

● The swimmer should perform core development training exercises such as crunches and planks as a regular part of their dryland/land training programme.

Chapter 7: Kicking & Pulling Drills

Introduction: As the name suggests, this chapter focuses on combination kicking and pulling drills.

The key components for effective kicking and pulling are:
● Kicking should be initiated from their thighs (quads), hamstrings and buttocks (glutes), using the largest muscles in the body to drive propulsion.
● There should be minimal knee bend, one of the most common faults while freestyle kicking.
● Kicking with a bent knee increases drag and uses the relatively smaller calf muscles.
● Their feet should be in a pointed (plantar flexion) position.
● Pulling should be performed with a high elbow on the recovery phase, to assist maximum stroke length.
● Although pull buoys can restrict the body's rotation, the swimmer should focus on achieving maximum stroke length.
● Their head should be in a horizontal and prone position, in line with their body and legs, looking at the bottom of the pool, whilst pulling.
● When breathing, they should have one goggle lens completely in the water and with the other goggle lens, they should look across the surface of the pool.
● Their feet should be in a pointed (plantar flexion) position.

7.1: Piggyback

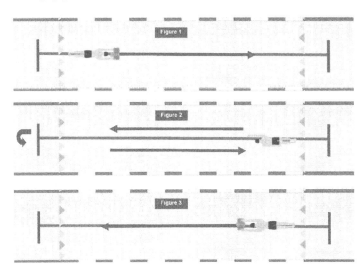

Purpose: This is an excellent introductory combination kicking and pulling drill.

How to perform this drill: This drill should be performed over four lengths of the pool (100m)

● The swimmer should start in the water and place a pull buoy on top of their kickboard.

● They should proceed from a push & glide off the wall at the end of the pool.

● They should ensure that they are holding their kickboard with fully extended arms.

● The swimmer should proceed to perform freestyle kicking for one length of the pool (25m). (figure 1)

● Without leaving the water, the swimmer should then place their kickboard on the poolside/deck, somewhere it can be easily retrieved.

● They then proceed to perform freestyle pulling with the pull buoy, for two lengths of the pool (50m). (figure 2)

● For the final 25m the swimmer should retrieve their kickboard and once again should place their pull buoy on top of their kickboard, and once again they should perform freestyle kicking for one length of the pool (25m). (figure 3)

● This drill can be performed as a recovery drill if required.

7.2: 'Tow your buddy'

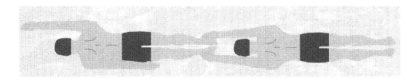

Purpose: The first in a series of intense kicking and pulling development drills.

How to perform this drill: The swimmer should pick a partner (buddy).

● This drill works better if the swimmers are roughly of the same size and ability.

● Both swimmers should start in the water, one in front of the other.

● The swimmer in front, should scull in a prone position (on their front) and lift their legs to the surface.

● The swimmer at the rear, should grab hold of both ankles of the swimmer in front.

● The left ankle in their left hand and the right ankle in their right hand.

● The swimmer in the front should then proceed to freestyle pull for a length of the pool (25m).

● While the swimmer at the rear proceeds to perform a freestyle leg kick, while still holding the ankles of the swimmer in front.

● The swimmers should change positions and repeat this drill for another length of the pool (25m)

7.3: 'Tow your buddies'– in a line

Purpose: This is the next in a series of kicking and pulling development drills.

How to perform this drill: The swimmers should work in threes for this drill.

● This drill works better if the swimmers are roughly of the same size and ability, with each swimmer in the water in a line.

● The swimmer in front, should scull in a prone position (on their front) and lift their legs to the surface.

● The swimmer at the middle, should grab hold of both ankles of

the swimmer in front.
- The left ankle in their left hand and the right ankle in their right hand.
- The swimmer in the middle should then lift their legs to the surface.
- The swimmer at the rear, should grab hold of both ankles of the swimmer in the middle.
- The left ankle in their left hand and the right ankle in their right hand.

- The swimmer in front should start this drill by performing a freestyle pull.
- The middle swimmer should raise themselves out of the water to breathe.
- While the swimmer at the rear proceeds to perform a freestyle leg kick while still holding the ankles of the swimmer in front.
- This drill should be conducted over three lengths of the pool (75m).
- The swimmers should change position every 25m, so that each swimmer, takes turns of performing this drill in each of the positions.

7.4: 'Tow your buddies' – two pulls, one kicks

Purpose: This is the next in a series of kicking and pulling development drills.

How to perform this drill: The swimmers should work in threes for this drill.

- This drill works better if the swimmers are roughly of the same size and ability.
- The swimmers should start in the water with two swimmers positioned in front and one swimmer positioned at the rear.
- The swimmer at the rear should hold the right ankle of the swimmer in front on the left and the left ankle of the swimmer in front on the right.

- The two swimmers at the front proceed by performing freestyle pulling, while the swimmer at the rear performs a freestyle leg kick.
- This drill should be conducted over three lengths of the pool (75m).
- The swimmers should change position every 25m, so that each swimmer, takes turns of performing this drill in each of the positions.

7.5: 'Tow your buddies' – one pulls, two kicks

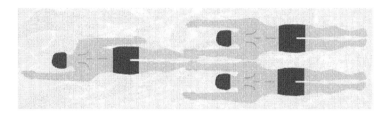

Purpose: This is the last in a series of kicking and pulling development drills.

How to perform this drill: The swimmers should work in threes for this drill.

- This drill works better if the swimmers are roughly of the same size and ability.
- The swimmers should start in the water with one swimmer in front and two swimmers at the rear.
- The swimmer at the rear on the left should hold the right ankle of the swimmer in front and the swimmer at the rear on the right should hold the ankle on the left of the swimmer in front.
- The swimmer at the front should perform freestyle pulling, while the swimmers at the rear should perform a freestyle leg kick.
- This drill should be conducted over three lengths of the pool (75m).
- The swimmers should change position every 25m, so that each swimmer, takes turns of performing this drill in each of the positions.

Chapter 8: Stroke Counting

Introduction: Stroke counting is a key swimming skill, which helps the swimmer develop and maintain a long, controlled, consistent and effective stroke.

● Stroke counting involves the swimmer counting the number of strokes (each time each hand enters the water) that they take to complete a given distance.

● Please note there is no one correct stroke count total, as swimmers are all shapes, sizes, abilities and strengths.

● Therefore, the number of strokes it takes to complete a certain distance is unique to each swimmer.

The key components for an effective stroke count are:
● A flat, horizontal and prone body position
● The head is in a horizontal and prone position, in line with their body and legs, looking at the bottom of the pool, whilst swimming.
● A low head position, with one goggle lens in the water, the other looking across the surface of the pool, whilst breathing.
● A smooth and controlled body rotation, which should be initiated from the shoulders, trunk and hips.
● Pulling with a high elbow recovery phase, to assist maximum stroke length
● Feet should be in a pointed (plantar flexion) position.
● A strong and steady freestyle (flutter) leg kick.

8.1: Establishing stroke count

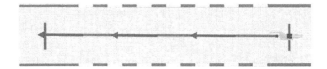

Purpose: This is the first in a series of stroke count drills, introducing the swimmer to establishing a stroke count.

How to perform this drill: The swimmer should start this drill from a push & glide from the wall at the end of the pool in a prone (face down) streamlined position.

• They should then proceed by performing full stroke freestyle for one length/lap of the pool at a steady pace, with great technique.

• The swimmer should count the number of strokes (each time each hand enters the water) they take to complete a length.

• When they have finished this drill, it's important to ensure that they allow the swimmers swimming behind them enough room to allow them to complete the drill.

8.2: Reducing stroke count

Purpose: This is the second in the series of stroke count drills, introducing the swimmer to reducing their stroke count.

How to perform this drill: This drill aims to reduce the swimmer's stroke count by at least one stroke, per length/lap.

• The swimmer should start this drill from a push & glide from the wall at the end of the pool in a prone (face down) streamlined position.

• They should then proceed by performing full stroke freestyle for one length/lap of the pool at a steady pace, with great technique

• They may reduce their stroke count by stronger kicking, stronger arm pulls, better underwater kicking from the start, a better technical stroke or a combination of all of these.

● When they have finished this drill, it's important to ensure that they allow the swimmers swimming behind them enough room to allow them to complete the drill.

8.3: Holding the stroke count

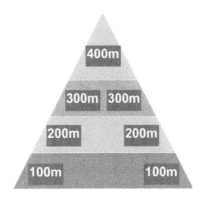

Purpose: This is the third in a series of stroke count drills, introducing the swimmer to holding their stroke count over a longer distance.

How to perform this drill: Once a regular stroke count has been established.

● The next stage is for the swimmer to 'hold' (maintain) their regular stroke count over a longer distance.

● This drill can be conducted over repeat sets of 100m/200m or, as I prefer, conducting a 'pyramid' in 100m steps i.e. 100m, 200m, 300m, 400m, 300m, 200m, 100m (steps of 50m for younger swimmers).

● The swimmer should start this drill from a push & glide from the wall at the end of the pool in a prone (face down) streamlined position.

● When they have finished this drill, it's important to ensure that they allow the swimmers swimming behind them enough room to allow them to complete the drill.

8.4: Stroke count with fists

Purpose: This is the fourth in a series of stroke count drills, introducing the swimmer to improving their stroke count by the introduction of swimming with clenched fists.

How to perform this drill: The swimmer should start this drill from a push & glide from the wall at the end of the pool in a prone (face down) streamlined position.

● They then proceed by performing full stroke freestyle for one length/lap of the pool at a steady pace, with great technique

● The swimmer should clench their fists and then go through the 'establishing' 'reducing' and 'holding' stroke count drills.

● When they have finished these drills, it's important to ensure that they allow the swimmers swimming behind them enough room to allow them to complete the drills.

● Often once the swimmer has completed these drills when they go back to normal stroke counting, they may find that they have developed a better 'feel for the water' and as a result may be able to reduce their stroke count still further.

8.5: Stroke count - min-max drill

4 x 50m	Rep 1			Rep 2			Rep 3			Rep 4		
	Stroke Coun			Stroke			Stroke			Stroke		
	t	Time	Total	Count	Time	Total	Count	Time	Total	Count	Time	Total
Swimmer 1	30	36	66	32	34	66	30	34	64	32	32	64
Swimmer 2	26	32	58	26	30	56	28	28	56	28	30	58
Swimmer 3	32	36	68	32	34	66	30	34	64	30	32	62
Swimmer 4	24	28	52	24	26	50	26	24	50	26	22	48

Purpose: This is the last in a series of stroke count drills.

● The objective of the min-max drill is to swim a given distance with the minimum amount of arm strokes with the maximum amount of speed.

How to perform this drill: For example, over 4 x 50m: A swimmer completes the first repetition in a time of 30 seconds with a stroke count of 36.

● By adding the number of seconds, it took to complete the set, to the number of strokes it took to complete the set, this gives the swimmer a total 'stroke efficiency score' of 66.

● The swimmer's objective for the next repetition is to reduce their stroke efficiency score by either swimming faster, taking fewer strokes or a combination of both. (see table above)

● When they have finished this drill, it's important to ensure that they allow the swimmers swimming behind them enough room to allow them to complete the drill.

Chapter 9: Aerobic Sets

Introduction: Aerobic conditioning* is the fitness 'cornerstone' of many swimming training programmes.
Aerobic conditioning (with air - endurance)

The key components for effective aerobic sets are:
● Long smooth steady swims, without the deterioration of technique.
● Long distance swims with short rest intervals, progressively increasing in intensity and/or distance, throughout the season.

9.1: Front to back swims

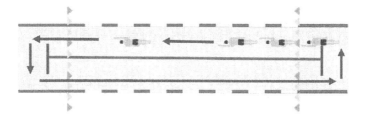

Purpose: This is an excellent aerobic drill, which requires the swimmer to swim at a sustained pace off the front of a slow-moving file of swimmers, to eventually re-join them at the rear of the file.
How to perform this drill: This drill is best performed by four to six swimmers per lane of roughly the same swimming ability.
● The swimmers should start this drill from a push and glide off the wall at the end of the pool.
● They should swim in a file (line), swimming at drill pace and ensuring that they are swimming very close to the swimmer in front, leaving a minimal gap.

- On a signal from the coach, the swimmer at the front, should then swim off the front of the file, at 200m race pace.
- They should swim away from the file of slow-moving swimmers and eventually re-joining the file at the rear.
- The coach has the responsibility of sending off the swimmers at regular intervals.
- They should ensure that at least two swimmers remain swimming slowly in the file.
- The swimmer at the front of the file should regularly look at the coach, to ensure they start their race pace swim at the correct time.
- It's also important that the swimmer at the front of the file does not speed up and keeps swimming at a drill pace.

9.2: Two-four-six-eight

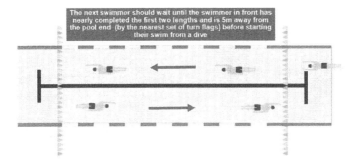

Purpose: Before performing this drill, attention should be paid to the swimmer's safety.
- The coach should ensure that all swimmers fully understand this drill, 'walking through it' if necessary.

How to perform this drill: This drill is best performed by four to six swimmers per lane, of roughly the same swimming ability.
- From a dive, the first swimmer in each lane should swim eight lengths of the pool (200m) @ 200m race pace.
- The next swimmer should wait until the first swimmer has nearly completed the first two lengths and is 5m away from the pool end (by the nearest set of turn flags).
- They then dive into the other side of the same lane and starts swimming for six lengths of the pool (150m) also @ 200m race pace.
- The next swimmer again should wait until the second swimmer has nearly completed their first two lengths and is 5m away from the pool end (by the nearest set of turn flags).

- They then proceed to enter the water via a dive and to swim for four lengths of the pool (100m) @ 200m race pace.
- The last swimmer again should wait until the second swimmer has nearly completed their first two lengths and is 5m away from the pool end (by the nearest set of turn flags).
- They then proceed to enter the water via a dive and to swim for two lengths of the pool (50m) @ 200m race pace
- This drill should be repeated four times until all the swimmers have swum all the different distances.
- If there are more than four swimmers in a team, swimmers can swim in pairs, requiring a pair to start their swim when the proceeding swimmer is 10m from the end of the pool or increase this drill to say a two-four-six-eight-ten-twelve.
- ***Please be careful when performing this drill.***
- ***It may require a walk-through explanation when first attempting this drill.***
- ***Ensure the swimmers stay focused on when they should dive into the water.***
- ***Remember safety first!***

9.3: 'T' 10's

Purpose: Timed swims are a great way of monitoring the aerobic fitness of your swimmers.
- They should be performed at regular intervals throughout the season.
- 'T' 10s are timed ten minutes swims.
- This drill has the objective of recording the number of lengths/laps a swimmer completes during this period.

How to perform this drill: The swimmer should start this drill from a push & glide from the wall at the end of the pool in a prone (face down) streamlined position.
- They then proceed to perform full stroke freestyle for the duration of this drill.
- The number of lengths/laps the swimmer completes during this

swim should be recorded and monitored against subsequent repetitions of this drill throughout the season.

Variation: Once mastered this set can be adjusted to fifteen minutes ('T' 15's) or twenty minutes ('T' 20's)

9.4: 500m challenge

Purpose: Some coaches prefer to test their swimmer's aerobic fitness over a given distance.

● They should be performed at regular intervals throughout the season

● This drill has the objective of recording the time it takes a swimmer to complete a given distance.

How to perform this test set: The swimmer should start this drill from a push & glide from the wall at the end of the pool in a prone (face down) streamlined position.

● They then proceed to perform full stroke freestyle for the duration of this drill.

● The swimmer should be timed to track how long it takes them to complete a 500m freestyle swim.

● This should be recorded and monitored against subsequent repetitions of this drill throughout the season.

● This 500m challenge should take most swimmers between 7 to 10 minutes.

Variation: Once mastered this set can be adjusted to a 1000m or 2000m challenge if required, which is great for long-distance swimmers.

9.5: Swim and pull set

	Lane 1(- 10 Seconds)	Lane 2 (-5 Seconds)	Lane 3 = 2 Minutes per100m
Swim 400m	7.20	7.40	8.00
Pull 100m	1.50	1.55	2.00
Swim 300m	5.30	5.45	6.00
Pull 200m	3.40	3.50	4.00
Swim 200m	3.40	3.50	4.00
Pull 300m	5.30	5.45	6.00
Swim 100m	1.50	1.55	2.00
Pull 400m	7.20	7.40	8.00

Purpose: This drill should be performed at regular intervals throughout the season.
• Swim and pull sets are a great way of monitoring the aerobic fitness of your swimmers.
How to perform this drill: The swimmer should start this drill from a push & glide from the wall at the end of the pool in a prone (face down) streamlined position.
• They then proceed to perform a series of full stroke freestyle and freestyle pull sets for the duration of this drill.
• The drill starts with a 400m swim, followed by a 100m pull.
• It proceeds with a 300m swim, followed by a 200m pull.
• It continues with a 200m swim, followed by a 300m pull.
• The drill finishes with a 100m swim, followed by a 400m pull.
• Swimmers should swim a total of 2000m as 1000m swim and 1000m pull.
The table above shows the suggested initial target times for different standards of swimmers.
• Lane 1 National/Top Regional Swimmers.
• Lane 2 Regional/Top County/State Swimmers.
• Lane 3 County/State/Club Swimmers.

Chapter 10: Sprinting

Introduction: Sprint training requires short bursts of speed at or near to the swimmer's maximum.

● It usually requires long rest intervals during and between sprint sets/reps, to allow the swimmer time to recover.

● For tougher sets swimmers may require 1-part work to 2-part rest: i.e. 15 seconds sprint work and 30 seconds rest/recovery.

● The major focus of sprinting should be on speed, without the deterioration of technique.

10.1: Sprint and recovery

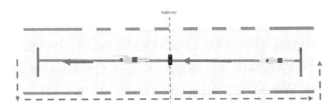

Purpose: This is an excellent drill for developing explosive sprinting.

● The swimmer should ensure that they perform their sprints to their maximum speed when required.

● They should ensure that they perform the recovery swim at a drill pace.

How to perform this drill: From a dive, the swimmer should sprint freestyle for half a length of the pool (12.5m).

● For the remainder of the length/lap they swim at a drill/recovery pace.

● At the end of the length/lap the swimmer should get out of the pool and walk slowly back to the other end of the pool.

● The walk back can be included as a part of their recovery.

- This drill should be introduced by repeating it four times.
- The number of reps can be increased once the swimmer begins to adapt to the workload.
- A sinker or a rubber brick on the bottom of the pool at halfway, would greatly assist the swimmer during this drill.

10.2: Trickle breathing sprinting

Purpose: This drill introduces the swimmer to trickle breathing while sprinting.

How to perform this drill: The swimmer should start this drill from a racing dive.

- They then proceed to freestyle sprint for one length/lap of the pool (25m).
- The swimmer should ensure that they take a large quick breath, which fills their lungs, while starting (diving off the block) and before they enter the water and start sprinting.
- The swimmer then slowly trickle breathes, intending to sprint the length/lap of the pool with as few breaths as possible.
- Once mastered, to add intensity, the swimmer may perform this drill with clenched fists
- Also see Chapter 4: Breathing Techniques.

10.3: Shooters drill

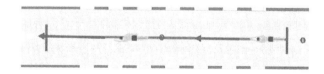

Purpose: To develop the swimmer's powerful underwater dolphin leg kick, explosive transition into the stroke and sprinting technique.
How to perform this drill: The swimmer should start this drill from a push & glide from the wall at the end of the pool, in a streamlined position.
● They should perform 10 underwater dolphin kicks then breakout to the surface (figure 1).
● The underwater dolphin kicks should be performed as quickly as possible.
● Once on the surface the swimmer should sprint freestyle for the remainder of the length/lap (25m) (figure 2)
● The breakout should be shallow enough to allow a smooth transition into a sprint freestyle.

10.4: Sprint from a dive then sprint from a push & glide

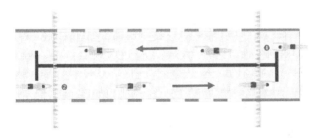

Purpose: This drill introduces the swimmer to a series of one length/lap sprints, at different intensities.
● This drill requires the swimmer to alternate their start of each sprint between starting from a dive and starting from a push and glide.
How to perform this drill: The swimmer should start this drill from a dive and sprint for one length/lap of the pool.
● The next sprint should be performed from a push & glide in the water, from the end of the pool, for one length/lap (25m).
● The 'odd' reps (1,3,5, etc) should be performed from a dive (preferably from a starting block) (figure 1).
● The 'even' reps (2,4,6, etc) should be performed from a push & glide in the water, from the end of the pool (figure 2).
● Each sprint is conducted on the same target time, which includes both the swim and the recovery.
● This gives the swimmer the advantage of diving on the odd reps, but then they should get out of the pool for the subsequent dive

repeats.
• On the even reps, the swimmer does not have to get out of the pool, but they don't have the advantage of a dive.
• Suggested number of introductory reps 6.
• Suggested introductory times: of 30secs for a 25m pool and 1 minute for a 50m pool.

10.5: Water polo freestyle

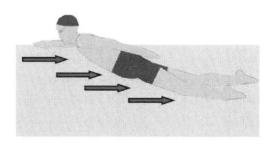

Purpose: This is a simple but effective, speed endurance drill for sprinters.

How to perform this drill: The swimmer should start this drill from a push & glide at the end of the pool, in a streamlined horizontal and prone position (on their front).

• They proceed to sprint for one length/lap of the pool, with their head fully out of the water.
• By raising their head, this should lower their legs in the water and should shorten the swimmer's stroke.
• The swimmer should keep their head upright and as still as possible.
• This should help to ensure that when performing this drill that there should be significant resistance to overcome.
• They should complete this drill for one length/lap of the pool (25m)

10.6: Sprint from back to front

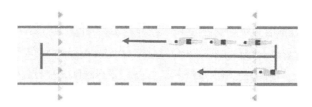

Purpose: This is an excellent intense sprinting drill.

How to perform this drill: This drill is best performed by four to six swimmers per lane, of roughly the same swimming ability.

● A single swimmer should start in the water on one side of a lane, at the end of the pool.

● The remaining swimmers should start on the other side of the lane, at the same end of the pool.

● The remaining swimmers should then proceed to swim freestyle at a drill pace, in a file (line) keeping to their side of the lane.

● They should swim as close to the swimmer in front as possible, with minimal gaps between each swimmer.

● When the leading file swimmer reaches approximately the 10m mark, the coach should signal the single swimmer to start sprinting.

● The objective is for the sprinter to pass all the slower swimmers in the file before the leading file swimmer reaches the end of the pool.

● The file swimmer should ensure that they do not speed up and remain swimming at a drill pace for the whole length.

● This drill should be repeated until all the swimmers have performed a sprint.

● Sprinters should recover by joining the slow swimmers at the end of the file, and therefore this drill should require a minimal rest interval.

● Coaches may need to adjust this drill for individual swimmers, to ensure the faster swimmers finish just ahead of the slower file swimmers.

10.7: Sprint with fins

Purpose: This drill helps to increase the swimmer's stroke rate.
How to perform this drill: The swimmer should start this drill, at

one end of the pool,
in a streamlined prone position (on their front) whilst wearing fins.
● The swimmer should proceed to sprint over a given distance.
● They should focus on performing a strong and quick leg kick.
● This should be initiated from the thighs, hamstrings and buttocks, using the largest muscles in the body to drive leg propulsion.
● Their feet should be in a pointed (plantar flexion) position.
● The tempo generated by wearing fins should naturally increase the swimmer's stroke rate.
● This can be an intense drill, that should be performed over short distances of no more than 25m, ideally 10m to 15m.

10.8: Bungee cord assisted freestyle

Purpose: This is another drill that helps to increase the swimmer's stroke rate.

How to perform this drill: This drill should be performed whilst the swimmer is towed by a tethered bungee cord.

● The cord should be comfortably and safely secured around the swimmer's waist, ideally via a belt.
● The swimmer should be towed by someone on the poolside/deck.
● The pace of the tow is important to the success of this drill.
● If the tow is too slow, the desired increase in arm speed may not be achieved.
● If the tow is too fast, the swimmer may not be able to feel or gauge any increase in arm speed.
● Therefore, this drill may take a few attempts to achieve the desired result.
● This can be an intense drill, that should be performed over short distances of no more than 25m, ideally 10m to 15m.

Chapter 11: Speed Play

Introduction: The introduction of varying speed swimming (speed play) into the freestyle stroke, helps to develop the swimmer's ability to swim at varying tempos.

● This type of training can be tough, but it can be an effective method of increasing a swimmer's fitness, speed and endurance.

The key components for effective speed play are:

● Swimming at varying speeds, without the deterioration of technique.

● There should be a clear distinction between fast and slow swimming

● Slow swimming should be conducted at drill pace, while fast swimming should be conducted at sprint pace.

● Speed play often requires a lot of effort at maximum, or near to maximum speed.

● Therefore, the swimmer may require more rest than usual.

● For tougher sets swimmers may require 2 parts work to 1-part rest: i.e. 1-minute speed play and 30 seconds rest.

11.1: Swim – builds

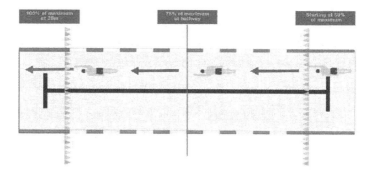

Purpose: This drill is an excellent introduction to swimming freestyle at varying speeds.

How to perform this drill: The swimmer should start this drill from a streamlined push and glide from the end of the pool.

● They should proceed by performing a steady full stroke freestyle.

● The swimmer should start swimming at approximately 50% of their maximum swimming speed and they should gradually increase the speed of their swim over one length.

● The swimmer should be swimming at approximately 75% of their maximum swimming speed at half-way.

● Without deterioration of technique, the swimmer should be close to reaching their maximum swimming speed as they approach the finish of the length/lap.

● The swimmer should ensure that they gradually increase both their arms and leg speed to increase the speed of their swim.

● Increasing their leg speed should naturally increase their arm speed.

● Younger and inexperienced swimmers may find it useful to use fins when first learning this drill.

11.2: Backend/frontend swims drills

Purpose: These drills introduce the swimmer to race pacing and tactics.
● For freestyle races of 100m or over, the swimmer should develop an idea of how they are best going to swim their race.
● There are two basic methods of pacing a race.
● The first is to start at a steady pace and build speed towards the end of the race (backend swims).
● The second is to start quickly and try to maintain a fast pace for as long as possible (frontend swims).

How to perform these drills - backend swims: This drill introduces the swimmer to swimming progressively faster over four lengths/laps of the pool (100m).
● The swimmer should start this drill from a push and glide for the wall at the end of the pool.
● They should proceed to swim full stroke freestyle at a steady pace.
● For the first length/lap (25m), this should be at approximately 70% of their maximum swimming speed.
● The second length/lap should be swum faster than the first length, at approximately 75% of their maximum swimming speed.
● The third length/lap should be quicker than the second length/lap, at approximately 80% of their maximum swimming speed.
● The last length/lap should be quickest of all, at their maximum swimming speed.
● Each of the swimmer's length/lap splits for this drill should be timed, recorded and if necessary adjusted.

- The coach should give feedback to the swimmer and future race pace target timings adjusted accordingly.
- **Please note:** the objective of this drill is controlled speed, with great technique.
- The swimmer should focus on a fast and smooth stroke.

How to perform this drill - frontend swims: This drill has the objective to help the swimmer to start fast and attempt to hold onto a fast pace, without too much drop off in time over four lengths/laps of the pool (100m).

- The swimmer should start this drill from a push and glide for the wall at the end of the pool.
- For the first length/lap (25m), this should be at approximately 80% of their maximum swimming speed.
- Each of the swimmer's length/lap splits for this drill should be timed, recorded and if necessary adjusted.
- The coach should give feedback to the swimmer and future race pace target timings adjusted accordingly.
- **Please note:** the objective of this drill is controlled speed, with great technique.
- The swimmer should focus on a fast and smooth stroke.

11.3: Race pace development set

Purpose: This is a great race pace set for developing the swimmer's ability to perform even-paced, frontend and backend swims.

- An even-paced swim: Swims that are performed at the same pace throughout the race.
- A frontend swim: Swims which are performed faster at the beginning of the race than at the end.

• A backend swim: Swims which are performed faster at the end of the race than at the beginning.

How to perform this set: The swimmer should start this drill from a push and glide for the wall at the end of the pool.

• This set should be performed as 6 x 300m broken swims.

• As a 200m at race pace, with a 15-second rest interval

• This should be followed by a 100m recovery swim with a one-minute rest interval.

Reps 1 & 2: Even paced swims.

Reps 3 & 4: Frontend swims.

Reps 5 & 6: Backend swims.

• Each of the swimmer's length/lap splits for this drill should be timed, recorded and if necessary adjusted.

• The coach should give feedback to the swimmer and future race pace target timings adjusted accordingly.

• **Please note:** the objective of this drill is controlled speed, with great technique.

• The swimmer should focus on a fast and smooth stroke.

11.4: Descending swims

Purpose: Descending swims are a great way for helping to develop the swimmers back end swims.

• They require the swimmer to perform each rep quicker than the previous.

How to perform this drill: The swimmer should start this drill by finding their optimum training pace for 100m. For example, 1.30 seconds.

• They should then perform 4 x 100m reducing each 100m rep by 3 seconds.

• For example, 1st) on 1.27 2nd) 1.24 3rd) 1.21 4th) 1.18

11.5: Speed play - easy/fast swims

Purpose: This drill helps to develop the swimmer's ability to swim at varying speeds.

How to perform this drill: The swimmer should start this drill from a streamlined push and glide from the end of the pool.

● They should proceed at a steady drill pace, with great technique for half a length.

● On reaching halfway, they should sprint for the remaining half of the length, without the deterioration of their technique.

● This drill can be reversed so that the swimmer sprints for half a length and swims at drill pace for the remaining half a length.

● A sinker or a rubber brick on the bottom of the pool at halfway, would greatly assist the swimmer during this drill.

11.6: Speed play - easy/fast strokes

Purpose: This drill helps to develop the swimmer's ability to swim short bursts at varying speeds.

How to perform this drill: The swimmer should start this drill from a streamlined push and glide from the end of the pool.

● They should proceed at a steady pace (200m race pace), with great technique for three strokes.

● The swimmer should then sprint for another three strokes, again without the deterioration of their technique.

● This drill should be repeated for a length of the pool (25m).

Variation: This drill can be adapted to increase the number of strokes i.e. five strokes easy/ five strokes fast.

● This drill can be a tough set for some swimmers, so any increase in distance should be carried out gradually and only once they have adapted to its demands.

● For tougher sets swimmers may require 2 parts work to 1-part rest: i.e. 1-minute speed play and 30 seconds rest.

11.7: Speed play set

Slow	Sprint
40m	10m
40m	10m
25m	25m
25m	25m
10m	40m
10m	40m

Purpose: This speed play drill should be conducted over a series of 50m sets.

How to perform this drill: The swimmer should start this drill from a streamlined push and glide from the end of the pool.

● They should perform a set of 6 x 50m off a suggested set time of one minute.

● The timings can be adjusted accordingly.

● The swimmer should swim at either drill pace (slow) or sprint pace (fast), at a varying distance over 50m.

● The first two sets should be performed as 40m slow or 10m fast.

● Sets three and four should be performed as 25m slow or 25m fast.

● The final two sets five and six, should be performed as 10m slow or 40m fast.

● Sinkers or rubber bricks at 10m from the end of each length and at halfway would greatly assist the swimmer during this drill.

11.8: Speed play swims – reducing times

1 x 25m on 30 seconds
2 x 25m on 25 seconds
1 x 25m on 30 seconds
2 x 25m on 20 seconds
1 x 25m on 30 seconds
2 x 25m on 15 seconds
1 x 25m on 30 seconds

Purpose: This is a great speed play drill of increasing intensity over 10 x 25m.

How to perform this drill: The swimmer should start this drill from a streamlined push and glide from the end of the pool.

● This drill starts with an easy-paced one length/lap swim on 30 seconds.

● This should be followed by two single lengths/laps on the reduced time of 25 seconds.

● This should be followed by another easy-paced one length/lap swim on 30 seconds.

● This should be followed by a further two single lengths/laps of further reduced times swims of 20 seconds.

● This should be followed by another easy-paced one/lap length swim on 30 seconds.

● The last two lengths/laps of reduced times swims should be performed at maximum speed on 15 seconds.

● This should be followed by a final an easy-paced one length/lap swim on 30 seconds.

Chapter 12: Streamlining

- The ability to perform an effective streamlined position is a key swimming skill.
- Effective streamlining can reduce drag and maintain the swimmer's speed and
the distance achieved during their starts, turns and breakouts*.
- Therefore, they should be regularly developed, practised and maintained, especially for younger or inexperienced swimmers.
Breakouts the phase at the end of a start or a turn, where the swimmer makes the transition into a full freestyle stroke.

How to perform an effective streamlined position
To perform an effective streamlined position, the swimmer should be in a long torpedo shape, where the fingers, hands, arms, head, body, legs and feet are on the same level plane.

Fingers
The swimmer's fingers should be closed and pointing in the direction they wish to travel.

Hands
Their hands should be placed on top of one another, with the thumb

of the upper hand wrapped around the outside of the lower hand, locking them into position.
● They should be pointing in the direction they wish to travel.

Arms

The swimmer's arms should be fully extended to narrow the shoulders.
● They should be pointing in the direction they wish to travel.
● There should be no bend at the elbows.
● To facilitate this, the swimmer's biceps should be squeezed tightly at the rear of the swimmer's head and not pressing against their ears.

Coach Arthur says: "When the swimmer is squeezing their biceps against their head, they should do so behind their ears.
● Not only is the head a little narrower there, which results in better streamlining, but by doing so it narrows the shoulders, resulting in a more effective streamlined position.
● Some coaches prefer for their swimmers to place their chin on their chest and squeeze their arms behind their head.
● I recommend trying both positions to see which one you prefer".

Head

● Their head should be in a neutral position in line with the swimmer's arms and body.

Body

Their body should be in a flat and horizontal position with the swimmer's core engaged.

Engaging a swimmer's core

Engaging the core muscles ensures that they are correctly aligned, to help support and perform certain swimming drills and skills effectively.
● To engage their core, the swimmer should continue to breathe normally.
● They should then tighten/contract their stomach muscles while drawing their navel towards their spine.

Core strength development

To effectively engage their core whilst performing underwater dolphin kicking, the swimmer should develop their core strength.
● They should perform core development training exercises such

as crunches and planks as a regular part of their dryland/land training programme.

Legs
The swimmer's legs should be straight and closed tightly together, with no bend at the knees.

Feet
Their feet should be in a pointed (plantar flexion) position, which reduces drag and places them in the optimum position for maximum propulsion.

12.1: Push & glide in the prone position

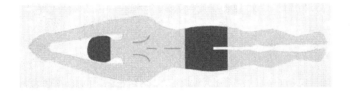

Purpose: This is a classic introductory streamlining drill.
How to perform this drill: The swimmer should start this drill from a push and glide from the wall at the end of the pool.
- They should focus on very tight streamlining.
- They should perform this drill about half a metre under the surface.
- They should attempt to get past the turn flags with their head (a good attempt) or their feet (a better attempt), before breaking out to the surface.
- They should ensure that they perform a strong push off the wall.
- The swimmer should ensure that they do not perform any kicking or body undulation movements.
- The coach should mark where the swimmer 'breaks out' on the surface on the poolside.

Coach Arthur says: To achieve an effective push and glide, the swimmer should ensure that their feet are firmly planted on the pool wall.
- Ideally shoulder-width apart and that their knees are bent at approximately ninety degrees.

12.2: Starfish drill

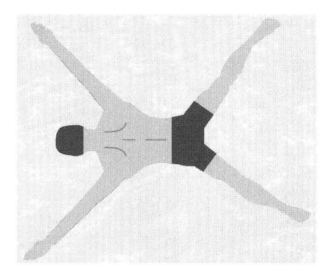

Purpose: This is an excellent drill for demonstrating the effectiveness of tight streamlining.

How to perform this drill: The swimmer should start this drill from a push and glide from the wall at the end of the pool, underwater in a streamlined prone position, about half a metre under the surface.

● As soon as the swimmer has left the wall, they should open both their arms and legs into a forty-five degrees position.

● This non-streamlined position should result in the swimmer coming to an almost complete stop in the water.

● This should demonstrate to the swimmer, the effectiveness of tight streamlining.

Chapter 13: Underwater Dolphin Kicking

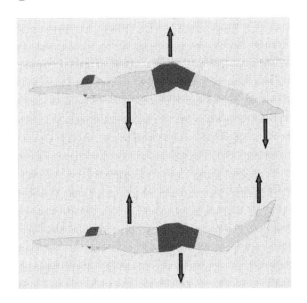

Introduction: Underwater dolphin kicking has become an increasingly important swimming skill, playing a key part in the development of freestyle starts and turns.

The key components for an effective underwater dolphin kick are:
● The propulsion should be initiated by a shallow 'head to toes' undulation of the swimmer's body.
● The swimmer should assume a streamlined position and engage their core.
● Legs are together and feet should be in a pointed (plantar flexion) position.
● This reduces drag and places their feet in the optimum position for maximum propulsion.
● The swimmer should ensure they are performing trickle breathing, to help them complete these drills (see Chapter 4: Breathing Technique).
● It may be beneficial for younger or less experienced swimmers to wear fins while they master these drills.

How to perform an underwater dolphin kick

- The swimmer should initiate a shallow body undulation from their head, through their chest, hips and their legs.
- They should start the undulation cycle by, pressing downwards with their head and chest, which raises their hips, which in turn lowers their legs.
- The downward leg kick provides a major propulsive force.
- The swimmer should complete the undulation cycle by raising their head and chest, which lowers the hips, which in turn naturally raises their legs.
- The swimmer should focus on fast, vigorous and shallow underwater dolphin kicks to generate speed.

13.1: Vertical underwater dolphin kicking

Purpose: This is a great introductory drill for underwater dolphin kicking.

How to perform this drill: A diving pit or a pool with a deep end, is a great place for a swimmer to learn and practice vertical underwater dolphin kicking.

● The swimmer should start this drill by sinking to the bottom of the pool.

● They should then adopt a streamlined squat position.

● They should then drive up through their legs and perform vigorous, vertical underwater dolphin kicking, to shoot through the water to the surface.

- The swimmer should ensure they are performing trickle breathing, to help them complete this drill.
- Once mastered the swimmer should try to increase the speed of their kicks.
- Younger and inexperienced swimmers may find it useful to use fins when first learning this drill.

13.2: Underwater dolphin kicking development

Purpose: This is a further introductory drill to help develop and maintain an effective underwater dolphin kick.

How to perform this drill: The swimmer should start this drill a push and glide from the end of the pool, about half a metre under the surface.

- They should commence with this dill by initially performing 6 underwater dolphin kicks, to help them gauge the distance they can travel underwater.
- Once mastered they should gradually increase the number of kicks until they can perform this drill over 15m.
- The swimmer should ensure they increase their speed while discovering how many underwater dolphin kicks it takes them to reach 15m.
- This is the maximum distance a swimmer can travel legally underwater after a start or a turn.
- A sinker or rubber brick on the bottom of the pool at 15m would greatly aid swimmers during this drill.
- The swimmer should ensure they are performing trickle breathing, to help them complete this drill (see Chapter 4: Breathing Technique).
- Younger and inexperienced swimmers may find it useful to use fins when first learning this drill.

Variations: Resistance can be added by the swimmer crossing their arms across their chest or folding their arms above their head while performing these drills.

13.3: Underwater dolphin kicking – corkscrewing

Purpose: This drill can further help to develop and maintain an effective underwater dolphin kick, by the introduction of 'corkscrewing' through the water, which is required during a turn.

How to perform this drill: The swimmer should start this drill from a push and glide from the end of the pool, approximately half a metre under the surface.

● The swimmer should then perform a 'corkscrew' dolphin kick.

● This is achieved by the swimmer kicking three underwater dolphin kicks on their front, three underwater dolphin kicks on their right-hand side, three underwater dolphin kicks on their back and three underwater dolphin kicks on their left-hand side.

● Once completed they should rise to the surface for a breath, then return to approximately half a metre under the surface and repeat this drill.

● The swimmer should initiate their body rotation from their shoulders, trunk and hips.

● The swimmer should ensure they are performing trickle breathing, to help them complete this drill (see Chapter 4: Breathing Technique).

● They should complete this drill for one length/lap of the pool (25m).

Variations: Resistance can be added by the swimmer crossing their arms across their chest or folding their arms above their head while performing these drills.

13.4: Sideways underwater dolphin kicking

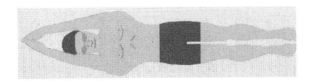

Purpose: This is an underwater dolphin kicking drill to help the swimmer to develop a powerful dolphin leg kick while on their side, which is required during a turn.

How to perform this drill:

● The swimmer should start this drill from a push and glide from the wall at the end of the pool.

● They should perform six underwater dolphin kicks on their right-hand side in a tight streamlined position, approximately half a metre under the surface.

● Once completed they should rise to the surface for a breath, then return to approximately half a metre under the surface and repeat the drill.

● The swimmer should ensure they are performing trickle breathing, to help them complete this drill.

● They should complete this drill for one length/lap of the pool (25m).

● They should repeat this drill by underwater dolphin kicking on their left-hand side.

Variations: Resistance can be added by the swimmer crossing their arms across their chest or folding their arms above their head while performing these drills.

13.5: Underwater dolphin kicking - tempo drill

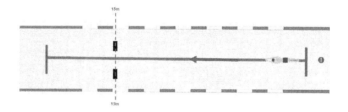

Purpose: This is an introductory underwater dolphin kicking speed development drill, which can help the swimmer establish the most effective tempo/speed of their kick.

● If a swimmer performs underwater dolphin kicks that are too big, then they may increase drag/resistance.

● However, if a swimmer performs underwater dolphin kicks that are too small, then they may not be an effective means of propulsion.

● The optimum underwater dolphin kick for most swimmers is somewhere in between.

How to perform this drill: The swimmer should start this drill from a push and glide from the wall at the end of the pool.

● They should then perform fast and vigorous underwater dolphin kicking over a distance of 15m (figure 1).

● The swimmer should count the number of underwater dolphin kicks they require to complete this distance.

● This is the maximum distance a swimmer can travel legally underwater after a start or a turn.

● The coach should record the time they take to complete this distance and feed this information back to the swimmer.

● The swimmer may need to adjust the depth of their kick and tempo until they achieve their optimum time.

● The swimmer should ensure they are performing trickle breathing, to help them complete this drill (see the chapter on breathing technique).

● Younger or less experienced swimmers may need to use fins when first learning this drill.

13.6: Underwater dolphin kicking - shooters drill

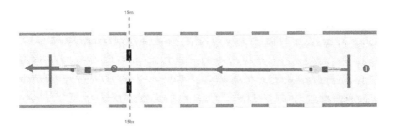

Purpose: This is an excellent drill for further developing and maintaining speed while underwater dolphin kicking.

How to perform this drill: The swimmer should start this drill from a streamlined push and glide from the wall at the end of the pool, about half a metre under the surface.

● The swimmer should then perform ten underwater dolphin kicks at maximum speed (figure 1).

● They should then breakout to the surface and sprint full stroke freestyle for the remainder of the length (25m) (figure 2).

● The underwater dolphin kicks should be performed as quickly as possible and the breakout should be shallow enough to allow a smooth transition into a sprint freestyle stroke.

● The swimmer should ensure they are performing trickle breathing, to help them complete this drill (see the chapter on breathing technique).

• Once mastered the swimmer should perform underwater dolphin kicks to 15m.

• This is the maximum distance a swimmer can travel legally underwater after a start or a turn.

• A sinker or rubber brick placed at 15m on the bottom of the pool would greatly assist this drill.

13.7: Underwater dolphin kicking - sprint drill

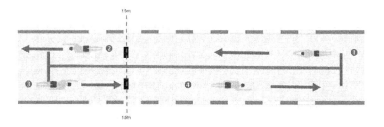

Purpose: This is an excellent drill for developing and maintaining speed and endurance, for both their underwater dolphin kicking and their full butterfly stroke.

How to perform this drill: Over two lengths (50m) with a sinker or a rubber brick at 15m at the bottom of the pool.

• The swimmer should start this drill from a streamlined push and glide from the wall at the end of the pool, about half a metre under the surface.

• They should then perform underwater dolphin kicking for 15m as fast as possible (figure 1)

• This is the maximum distance a swimmer can travel legally underwater after a start or a turn.

• At 15m the swimmer should rise to the surface and swim an easy freestyle to the end of the pool, where they perform a freestyle tumble/flip turn (figure 2)

• Once out of the turn, the swimmer continues to swim an easy freestyle for a further 10m (figure 3).

• At the 15m mark the swimmer sprints full stroke freestyle to the end of the pool (figure 4).

• A sinker or rubber brick placed at 15m on the bottom of the pool would greatly assist this drill.

13.8: Underwater dolphin kick relay

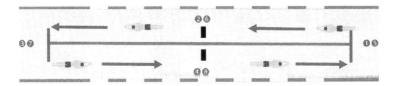

Relay objective: This relay conducted over a short distance, helps to develop the swimmer's underwater dolphin kicking speed/tempo.

Team criteria: Two or more teams, of two to eight swimmers, of roughly the same ability and speed.

Equipment required: Two rubber bricks/sinkers per lane and a poolside marker at half-way.

Relay preparation: All swimmers should start this relay in the water.

● Two rubber bricks or sinkers should be placed at half-way. One on each side of the lane.

● A poolside marker should be placed at half-way, to help ensure that the rubber bricks/sinkers are correctly positioned.

● Each team should position a swimmer at both ends of the pool and on both sides of the lane in the middle of the pool.

● If there are more than four swimmers per team, the fifth swimmer should join the swimmer at the starting end of the pool

● The sixth swimmer should join the swimmer at the right-hand side of the lane in the middle of the pool

● The seventh swimmer should join the swimmer at the other end of the pool.

● The eighth swimmer should join the swimmer at the right-hand side of the lane in the middle of the pool.

Relay description: From the starting end of the pool, the first swimmer should perform a push and glide and performs a fast underwater dolphin kick, **DOWN THE RIGHT-HAND SIDE OF THE LANE.**

● They should proceed to half-way, where they should change to the second swimmer by touching hands

● The second swimmer should then perform a fast underwater dolphin kicking to the other end of the pool.

● The third swimmer should then perform a fast underwater dolphin kicking to the middle of the pool, **DOWN THE RIGHT-HAND SIDE OF THE LANE**.

● The fourth swimmer in the middle of the pool should then quickly

underwater dolphin kick, back to the starting end of the pool.
- The winning team being those who completed the required number of underwater dolphin legs the quickest.

 Safety message: Please ensure that all swimmers are fully briefed and understand what is expected of them during any training relay. Remember safety first.

Chapter 14: Starts

Introduction: Many races, especially sprints, are lost even before the swimmer has entered the water, due to a poorly executed start.
● The development of a fast, explosive, racing start with distance, is a key objective for all competitive swimmers.

Key phases for an effective racing start are:
The freestyle start has three distinct phases: **off the block, the entry and the breakout.**

Phase 1: Off the block
This is the fastest part of the start, the explosive movement where the swimmer's feet leaves the block.
● The swimmer should have a solid starting position, leaning forward on the balls of their feet.
● They should react quickly to the starting signal (gun, bleep, etc.)
● The swimmer should be explosive off the block, driving through their thighs, legs, balls of their feet and big toes.
● They should thrust their arms forward off the block, into a streamlined position, which should be maintained on entry into the water.

Phase2: The entry

The entry into the water should be in a tight streamlined position.

• As soon as the swimmer enters the water, they should maintain the speed of their start by commencing with fast and vigorous underwater dolphin kicking.

• The rules allow for 15m of underwater dolphin kicking before the swimmer's head must break the surface.

Phase 3: The breakout

• The swimmer should rise parallel and just below the surface.

• The swimmer should keep one arm in the streamlined position.

• With the other arm they should perform a deep, fast and full stroke.

• Whilst doing so they should change their leg kick to a freestyle (flutter) kick.

• The swimmer should ensure that their head remains still and in a streamlined position.

• This should ensure that the swimmer's momentum should be forwards and not upwards, as this can significantly reduce drag.

• They should then breakout to the surface.

• To maintain momentum, on breaking out to the surface, the swimmer should not take a breath for two full strokes.

There are two types of competitive starts, the track start and the grab start.

Key components for an effective track start are:

• The swimmer should have a solid starting position, leaning forward on the balls of their feet.

• They should be explosive off the block, driving through their thighs, balls of their feet and big toes.

- The entry into the water should be streamlined to avoid drag.
- The depth of the dive should be shallow enough to ensure the speed of dive is maintained, but deep enough to allow a series of underwater dolphin kicks.
- The swimmer should maintain a fast, streamlined and efficient underwater dolphin kicking, looking to break out just before 15m.
- The rules allow for 15m of underwater dolphin kicking before the swimmer's head must break the surface.
- They should perform an effective break out into a full freestyle stroke without losing momentum.

How to perform a track start

- The swimmer should place one foot in front of the other.
- Most swimmers put their stronger leg in the back position.
- The swimmer's feet should be approximately shoulder-width apart.
- The swimmer should be stable on the block and their weight should be distributed evenly between their front and back legs.
- They should curl the toes of the leading foot over the edge of the block, enabling them to push off the block with maximum force.
- The swimmer's head should be tucked down, with their chin resting on their chest.
- They should have their hips as high as possible.
- The swimmer's centre of gravity should be positioned at the edge of the block.
- Their arms should be extended forward and grabbing hold of the front edge of the starting block with both hands.
- This should enable them to pull themselves off the block with maximum force.

Key components for an effective grab start are:

- The swimmer should place their feet approximately 15cms (6 inches) apart.
- They should be in a stable position on the starting block by distributing the weight in their legs evenly.
- The swimmer should curl their toes over the edge of the block, enabling them to push off the block with maximum force.
- The swimmer's head should be tucked down, as close to their knees as possible.
- Their hips should be as high as possible.
- The swimmer should place their hands either inside or outside of their feet, whichever they find most comfortable.
- The swimmer's centre of gravity should be positioned at the edge of the starting block.

14.1: Poolside/Deck 'blast' jump

Purpose: This is an excellent poolside/deck introductory drill which demonstrates the explosive power required for a competitive start.

How to perform this drill: The swimmer should ensure that they find a safe space on the poolside/deck away from the pool's edge.

● The swimmer should start this drill, by squatting down on the balls of their feet, with their hands by their side touching the poolside/deck floor.

● On the command 'jump', the swimmer should perform an explosive jump upwards by extending their arms, legs and feet, into a tight streamlined position.

● They should ensure that they drive from the thighs, through their lower legs and finally from the balls of their feet through to their toes.

14.2: Finding the balancing point

Purpose: Often younger or inexperienced swimmers when starting to learn how to perform a competitive start, find it difficult to locate their ideal starting position on the block.

● This is the first in a series of drills to help find the swimmer's 'balancing point' on the starting block.

● The balancing point is the position where they are steady enough to ensure they are still before the starting signal, but balanced ready to blast quickly off the starting block to achieve a fast reaction time.

How to perform this drill: The swimmer should start this drill by assuming their preferred starting position on the starting block.

● In the swimmer's own time, they should roll forward on the balls of their feet, until they feel they cannot go forward any more without falling into the water but are in a stable starting position (their balancing point).

● They should then roll back to their original starting position.

14.3: The balancing point with a dive

Purpose: This is the next in a series of drills to develop the swimmer's competitive start, by adding a dive to the 'balancing point' drill.

How to perform this drill: The swimmer should start this drill by finding their balancing point.

● They should then roll back on the block, then again, they should roll forward to find their balancing point.

● They should then perform a racing dive.

● They should ensure that they drive from the thighs, through their lower legs and finally from the balls of their feet through to their toes.

● They should also ensure that they thrust their arms forward off the block, into a streamlined position, which should be maintained on entry into the water.

14.4: Racing starts development

Purpose: The last in a series of drills to develop an effective competitive start.

How to perform this drill: The swimmer starts this drill by finding their balancing point.

- Then in their own time they should perform a racing dive off the blocks.
- To achieve a shallow racing dive, the swimmer should explode outwards off the racing blocks.
- If the swimmer dives too deep, it may be that the swimmer is not driving outwards off the starting block, but instead, they are driving downwards.
- If a swimmer looks down towards the bottom of the pool throughout the driving phases of their start, then this sometimes results in the dive being too deep.
- If the swimmer can lift their head for a split second, then quickly returns it to the streamlined position, during the driving phase of their start, then this sometimes results in a shallower dive.
- Another common fault, resulting in a deep racing dive, is the swimmer's hands position.

If the swimmer's hands are pointing downwards towards the bottom of the pool, this sometimes results in a deeper dive.

- As the swimmer locks their hands into a streamlined position off the block, they should slightly raise the tips of their fingers, which raises their hands slightly, which may result in the dive being performed to the correct depth.
- The coach should give the swimmer feedback, regarding any technical adjustments that may be needed, and praise the good aspects of their start.

14.5: Kick count starts

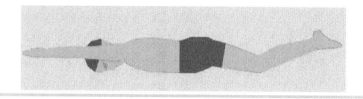

Purpose: To develop the swimmer's start by focusing on their underwater dolphin kicking technique.

How to perform this drill: The competitive swimming rules allow for 15m of underwater dolphin kicking before the swimmer's head must break the surface.

- Please note that this drill should deliver both speed and distance for this drill to be effective.
- The swimmer should start this drill by performing their preferred racing dive.
- They should count the number of kicks it takes to reach 15m.
- A sinker or a rubber brick on the bottom of the pool at 15m, would greatly assist the swimmer during this drill.
- This drill may take some time to master.
- For younger or less experienced swimmers, it may be advisable to start at a shorter distance, say 10m.

14.6: Breakout development drill

Purpose: This drill helps to further develop a swimmer's breakout from their underwater dolphin kicks into their full stroke.

How to perform this drill: The swimmer should start this drill by performing a racing dive.

- The swimmer should count the number of underwater dolphin kicks they take before they start to lose the momentum from the dive.
- By which time they should have ideally risen parallel and just below the surface.
- The swimmer should keep one arm in a streamlined position.
- With the other arm they should perform a deep, fast and full stroke.
- Whilst doing so they should change their leg kick to a freestyle (flutter) kick.
- The swimmer should ensure that their head remains still and in the streamlined position.
- This should ensure that the swimmer's momentum should be forwards and not upwards, as this could significantly reduce drag.
- They should then breakout to the surface.
- To maintain momentum, on breaking out to the surface, the swimmer should not take a breath for two full strokes.
- A sinker or a rubber brick at 15m would greatly assist this drill.

14.7: Timed starts

Purpose: This drill helps to further develop an effective competitive start, by the timing and recording of the swimmer's start.

How to perform this drill: The swimmer should start this drill by performing a race paced start.

● The coach should stand at the poolside/deck at 15m where a marker should be placed.

● As the swimmer passes the marker with their head, the coach should stop their stopwatch and record the result.

● The coach should give the swimmer feedback, regarding the time achieved, also any technical adjustments that may be needed and praise the good things about their start.

● A sinker or a rubber brick at 15m would greatly assist this drill.

Chapter 15: Turns

Introduction: One of the key technical areas in swimming is the ability to perform a freestyle 'tumble/flip' turn efficiently.

● So much time, distance and energy can be saved by the execution of an effective turn, that turn drills should be a regular part of any training programme.

The key components for an effective freestyle turn are:

- A fast approach, the swimmer should maintain their race speed, going into the wall.
- They should ensure that they take a big explosive breath as they swim into their turn. (see Chapter 4: Breathing Techniques)
- They should perform their tumble/flip turn quickly with their chin tucked in, their knees should be pulled up to the stomach and they should perform a full and forceful arm pull to help with a fast rotation.
- Their feet when planted on the pool wall, should be shoulder-width apart
- They should perform a strong, vigorous and streamlined push off the wall.
- The streamlining off the wall, should be as tight as the swimmer can achieve.
- They should undertake fast and vigorous underwater dolphin kicking, as soon as the swimmer completes their push off the wall.
- They should perform a fast 'corkscrew' rotation of the swimmer's body from their back to their front
- They should perform a fast, shallow and smooth breakout, ensuring that the swimmer has an efficient transition into their

stroke.
● The swimmer should not breathe for the first two strokes out of the turn, to help maintain their momentum.

15.1: Push & glide in the prone position

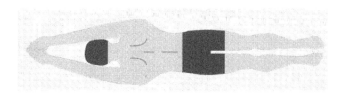

Purpose: This is an introductory drill to streamlining, an important skill in developing an effective turn.

How to perform this drill: The swimmer should start this drill by performing a vigorous push and glide off the wall at the end of the pool, in a tight streamlined position, about a metre under the surface.

● They should attempt to get past the turn flags before breaking out to the surface.

● If the swimmer breaks out with their head past the turn flags, this is a good attempt.

● If the swimmer breaks out with their feet past the turn flags, this is an excellent attempt.

● The coach should mark where the swimmer 'breaks out' to the surface on the poolside.

● The swimmer should perform trickle breathing while executing this drill.

Variation: As a contrasting activity, ask your swimmer to perform a push and glide in the least streamlined position they can.

● This should help to emphasise the importance of good streamlining.

15.2: Push & glide with underwater dolphin kicking

Purpose: A drill adding underwater dolphin kicking to streamlining, an important combination of skills in further developing an effective turn.

How to perform this drill: The swimmer should start this drill from a push & glide off the wall at the end of the pool, in a streamlined prone position, about a metre under the surface.

● Three vigorous underwater dolphin kick should commence as soon as the swimmer completes the push off the wall.

● This should result in the swimmer moving faster and further down the pool past the turn flags.

● The swimmer should perform trickle breathing while executing this drill.

● The coach should again mark where the swimmer 'breaks out' to the surface on the poolside and compare the difference between this and the drill above.

15.3: Push & glide on your side with underwater dolphin kick

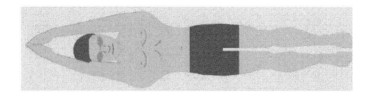

Purpose: This drill introduces the swimmer to the rotation of their body's shoulders, trunk and hips while performing an underwater dolphin kick.

How to perform this drill: The swimmer should start this drill from a push & glide off the wall at the end of the pool, in a streamlined prone position on their side, about a metre under the surface

● The swimmer should then rotate onto their front, by rotating their body, initiated from their shoulders, trunk and hips, while performing five quick underwater dolphin kicks, without losing both speed and distance.

● Again, the coach should mark where the swimmer 'breaks out' to the surface on the poolside.

● The swimmer should perform trickle breathing while executing this drill.

15.4: Push & glide supine with underwater dolphin kick + corkscrew

Purpose: This drill further develops the rotation of the swimmer's body's while performing underwater dolphin kicking.

How to perform this drill: The swimmer should start this drill from a push & glide off the wall at the end of the pool, in a streamlined prone position on their back, about a metre under the surface.

● The swimmer should then perform a 'corkscrew' dolphin kick.

● This is achieved by the swimmer kicking three underwater dolphin kicks on their front, three underwater dolphin kicks on their right-hand side, three underwater dolphin kicks on their back and three underwater dolphin kicks on their left-hand side.

● Once completed they should rise to the surface for a breath, then return to approximately half a metre under the surface and repeat this drill.

● The swimmer should initiate their body rotation from their shoulders, trunk and hips.

● The swimmer should ensure they are performing trickle breathing, to help them complete this drill (see Chapter 4: Breathing Technique).

● They should complete this drill for one length/lap of the pool (25m).

15.5: Mid-pool Turns

Purpose: This drill helps to develop a fast tumble/flip turn off either hand.

How to perform this drill: The swimmer should start this drill from a push & glide off the wall at the end of the pool, in a streamlined

prone position (on their front).
● The swimmer proceeds with this drill by swimming at 200m race pace.
● They should perform a series of mid-pool tumble/flip turns, down the length/lap of the pool, every five strokes.
● This helps to develop the swimmer's ability to be able to perform tumbles off either hand.
● While performing a mid-pool tumble/flip turn, the swimmer should quickly tuck their chin into their chest, pull their knees up to the stomach, tuck their heels up to their bottom and perform a deep and strong and fast single-arm pull to assist the rotation of the body in a tight tucked position.
● The swimmer should ensure that they have enough space in the lane to perform this drill correctly and are not rushed by other swimmers.

15.6: Tumbles against the wall

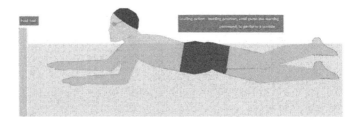

Purpose: This drill helps to develop a fast turn off the pool wall.
How to perform this drill: The swimmer should start this drill from approximately half a body length away from the wall at the end of the pool.
● They should hold their position while sculling and freestyle flutter kicking.
● On a signal from the coach, the swimmer should attempt to perform a tumble/flip turn as quickly and as perfectly as they can.
Variations: Once mastered, the swimmer should perform an effective push-off the pool wall with effective streamlining, attempting to clear the turn flags.
● They can later add five underwater dolphin kicks, looking to increase their distance off the wall.

15.7: Push & glide with breakout

Purpose: This drill further develops a fast turn by developing the swimmer's transition into their stroke.

How to perform this drill: The swimmer should start this drill from a push and glide from the wall at the end of the pool.

• They should begin to perform an underwater dolphin for five leg kicks.

• This should be performed approximately 0.5m (1 ½ foot) under the surface.

• At this depth it should allow the swimmer to quickly get into their stroke without having to stretch upwards.

• They should then breakout to the surface.

• Although most of the swimmer's head should be above the water, they should ensure that their face is in the water when they breakout.

• This should ensure that the swimmer's momentum should be forwards and not upwards, as this can significantly reduce drag.

• The swimmer should perform trickle breathing while executing this drill

• They should ideally take two full strokes, before taking their first breath.

15.8: Tumbles against the wall with breakout

Purpose: A further drill to develop a fast turn off the pool wall.

How to perform this drill: The swimmer should start this drill from approximately half a body length away from the wall at the end of the pool.

• They should hold their position while sculling and freestyle flutter kicking.

• On a signal from the coach, the swimmer should attempt to

perform a tumble/flip turn as quickly and as perfectly as they can.

● The swimmer should perform an effective push-off the pool wall with effective streamlining, and five underwater dolphin kicks, attempting to clear the turn flags.

● They should ensure that they perform an efficient transition into their stroke, at a depth approximately 0.5m (1 ½ foot) that should allow them to quickly get into their stroke without having to stretch upwards, as this may lose their momentum out of the turn.

● They should ensure they don't breathe on the first two strokes out of the turn, as this may also lose the momentum.

15.9: Timed turns

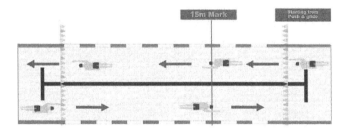

Purpose: This drill helps to further develop an effective turn, by the timing and recording of the swimmer's turn.

How to perform this drill: The swimmer should start this drill, in the water at the wall at the far end of the pool.

● The coach should stand at the poolside/deck, again 15m away from the turn end wall, where a marker or sinker should be placed on the poolside/deck and the pool bottom

● From a push and glide from the wall at the end of the pool, the swimmer should perform this drill, swimming at 100m race pace.

● As the swimmer's head passes the marker 15m from their turn, the coach should start their stopwatch.

● Once the swimmer has performed their turn and has swum back past the 15m marker the coach should stop the stopwatch, record the result and feed the result back to the swimmer.

15.10: Turns relay

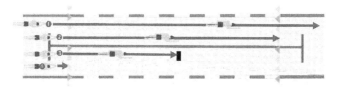

Purpose: A competitive drill to further help develop an effective turn, by performing mid-pool and race pace tumbles/flip turns under the pressure of a competitive relay.

How to perform this drill: This drill should work best if there are two or more teams of four to six swimmers, which are roughly the same ability and speed.

● Each swimmer should perform four turns over the distance of 125m.

● From a dive the swimmer should perform their first turn at the end of the pool (25m) (figure 1).

● They should then swim back to the starting end where they perform another turn.

● The swimmer should then perform a mid-pool turn at the far turn flags (20m) (figure 2).

● They should then swim back to the starting end where they perform another turn.

● The swimmer should then perform a mid-pool turn at the middle of the length (12.5m) (figure 3).

● They should then swim back to the starting end where they perform another turn.

● The swimmer then performs their final mid-pool turn at the nearest turn flags (5m) (figure 4).

● They should then swim back to the starting end where they finish their relay leg and another swimmer takes over.

● This series of turns should be repeated throughout the team until everybody in the team has swum.

● Placing rubber bricks or sinkers in each lane under both turn flags and at halfway would greatly assist this exercise.

Chapter 16: Finishes

Introduction: Many medals are lost, and personal best times are not achieved, due to poor finishing.

● As for all key swimming skills, finishing drills should be a regular part of any training programme.

The key components for an effective race finish are:
● The swimmers should maintain a fast approach.
● There should be no breathing from the turn flag to the end of the pool.
● They should finish with a fast and controlled, lateral body rotation, finishing with either arm in a fully extended 'catch' position which lengthens the stroke.
● They should aim to touch the '+' on the pool wall.
● There should be no head lift before touching the wall, which increases drag and shortens stroke.
● The swimmer should not glide into the wall.
● They should maintain a strong and fast leg kick.

16.1: Mid-Pool Finishing

Purpose: This drill helps develop the swimmer's ability to finish effectively on either hand.

- One of the key skills to be mastered when finishing is for the swimmer to finish with either arm in a fully extended 'catch' position.
- This enables the swimmer to slice through the water quickly, thus reducing drag and facilitating a longer stroke into the wall.

How to perform this drill: The swimmer should start this drill from a push & glide at the end of the pool.

- They should proceed to perform a full freestyle stroke at 200m race pace.
- They should swim for five freestyle arms strokes (each time the hand enters the water)
- Then they should quickly rotate their body and fully extend their right arm, into the catch position.
- They should place their left arm by their side, whilst placing their head on their extended right arm and gliding for three seconds
- This drill should be repeated, while alternating arms, for a length/lap of the pool (25m).

16.2: Timed finishes

Purpose: This drill helps to further develop an effective racing finish by the timing and recording of the swimmer's finish.

How to perform this drill: The swimmer should start this drill, from a push and glide from the wall at the far end of the pool, at 100m race pace.

- The coach should stand at the poolside/deck, 15m away from the turn end wall, where a marker or sinker should be placed on the poolside/deck and the pool bottom.
- As the swimmer's head passes the marker 15m from their turn, the coach should start their stopwatch
- Once at the 'T', at the end of the black line at the bottom of the pool, the swimmer should lunge for the '+' on the pool wall.
- The swimmer should ensure they have rotated their body and their finishing arm is in the fully extended catch position.
- They should start and finish this drill using alternate hands.
- Once the swimmer has performed their finish the coach should

stop their stopwatch, record the result and feed the result back to the swimmer.

• Once mastered, the swimmer should ensure that they don't take a breath from the turn flags until they have completed their finish.

16.3: Starts, turns and finish relay

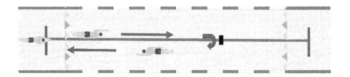

Purpose: A competitive drill to help further develop effective starts, turns and finishes.

How to perform this drill: This drill should work best if there are two teams or more of four to six swimmers, which are roughly the same ability and speed.

• The first swimmer on the starting signal, should perform a racing dive and then proceed to reach the 15m marker by the quickest means possible via a combination of underwater dolphin kicking and race pace swimming.

• The swimmer then performs a race pace mid-pool turn and then swims back to the start end of the pool where they perform a race pace finish.

• The next swimmer then performs a relay takeover.

• This process should be repeated throughout the team until everybody in the team has swum.

• Placing a rubber brick or sinker at 15m would greatly assist this drill.

Chapter 17: Warm-Ups & Cool-downs

Introduction: The importance of effective warm-ups and cool-downs is well documented, although it is still an area often overlooked in many training programmes.
● Before training and competition, the swimmer's muscles should be warmed, and their heart should be prepared to enable it to pump oxygen-rich blood throughout their body.
● After training and competition, the swimmer should perform an effective cool-down to aid muscle repair and help their recovery between training sessions or competition.
● It's, therefore, important to the swimmer's performance, to develop individual warm-up and cool-down protocols, which can be tailored to the individual swimmer and adapted to most training or competitive situations.

Examples of training and competition warm-up and cool-down protocols:

Warm-up 1: Dry Land Warm-up (Blood flow stretching):
● Usually conducted on the poolside/deck before entering the water.
● This is to help ensure that the swimmer's muscles have an adequate blood supply and are warm and supple before swimming.
Warm-up 2: The short pool warm-up:
● Sometimes swimmers only get a few minutes to warm-up in the pool.
● Therefore, it's important that the swimmer has developed an effective pre-planned short pool warm-up protocol.
● **Warm-up 3: The Championship pool warm-up:**

- When competing at a major event the swimmer usually gets up to an hour in the water to warm-up.

Warm-up 4: Pre-Race Warm-up (Blood flow stretching)
- A swimmer could have to wait for an hour or before their event.
- Therefore, it's important that the swimmers wake up their muscles and help increase the blood flowing through their body again.
- Ideally, this should be a 10-minute routine before the call up to their race.

Cool-down 1: Post Competition Swim Down:
- After any intense swimming activity, the swimmer's body and their nervous systems need time to repair and recover.
- Usually, the sooner the swimmer conducts their swim down the more effective the cool-down.

Cool-down 2: Post Competition Cool-down (Blood flow stretching).
- Swim down facilities are not always available at every meet/gala.
- Swimmers should get into the habit of stretching, walking or skipping after their race, to help their body and nervous system repair and recover.

Key components for a warm-up, cool-down and recovery swims are:
- Slow, smooth and controlled swimming
- They should include stroke counting, drills and speed play.
- The swimmer should keep moving during their warm-up to ensure their muscles are properly warmed up and their blood starts to flow.

17.1: American warm-up drill – strokes

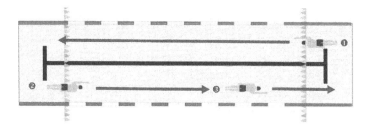

Purpose: This is an excellent warm-up drill, which requires the swimmer to perform a required number of strokes at a varying pace.
How to perform this drill: The swimmer should start this drill from a push & glide at the end of the pool.
- The swimmer proceeds with this drill by performing eighteen

strokes (each time the swimmer's hand enters the water) at drill pace, with their best technique (figure 1).

● They should then perform twelve strokes building to a 200m race pace (figure 2).

● Finally, they should perform six strokes holding a 200m race pace (figure 3).

● This drill should be repeated of the distance of 200m has been completed.

17.2: American warm-up drill – distance

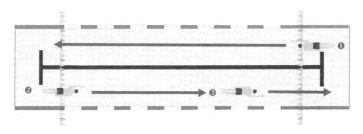

Purpose: This is an excellent warm-up drill, which requires the swimmer to swim certain distances at a varying pace.

How to perform this drill: The swimmer should start this drill from a push & glide at the end of the pool.

● The swimmer proceeds with this drill by performing 75m at drill pace, with their best technique (figure 1).

● They should then perform 50m building to a 200m race pace (figure 2).

● Finally, they should perform 25m holding a 200m race pace (figure 3).

● This drill should be repeated of the distance of 200m has been completed.

17.3: Super slow swimming

Purpose: Super slow swimming is an excellent cool-down drill to relax the swimmer and help them refocus on their technique.

How to perform this drill: The swimmer should start this drill from a push & glide at the end of the pool.

● The swimmer should proceed with this drill by swimming as slowly as they can, with their best technique.

● This drill should be completed for one length/lap of the pool (25m).

Variation: The swimmer can add stroke counting to their super slow swimming, to add extra focus to the length of their stroke.

Chapter 18: A Swimming Glossary

Introduction: Our swimming glossary contains a list of common competitive swimming terms with definitions, together with abbreviations and cross-references.

A

Aquatics: The collective (generic) name for any water-based competitive activity such as swimming, para-swimming, synchronised swimming, open water and water polo.

Aerobic Energy: The body's energy-producing system that requires oxygen.

Aerobic Training: The training system that requires oxygen. Usually involving long-distance swimming at a low intensity and a short rest interval.

Age Group Swimmers: Usually refers to swimmers under 16 years of age.

Anaerobic Energy: The body's energy-producing system that doesn't require oxygen.

Anaerobic Training: The training system that doesn't require oxygen. Usually involving short distance swimming at a high intensity and a long rest interval.

Anchor Leg: The final swimmer in a relay team.

Anchor Point: The point at the beginning of a stroke where the swimmer's hand starts to pull or push against the water at the beginning of the propulsive phase of the stroke.

Annual Training Plan: Usually formulated by the Head Coach during the closed season, this is an overall plan detailing the major objectives, championships and galas/meets for the up and coming season. It also outlines the different training periods for the season, together with an outline of what types of training activities should be performed.

Arm Stroke: The completion of an individual arm cycle, consisting of the pull phase, the exit phase and the recovery phase, before returning to the catch position at the start of the stroke.

Artistic Swimming see *Synchronised Swimming*

Ascending: Training set or rep on increasing times. Requiring a slower swim.

Assisted Training: Aided training that helps the swimmer go faster than normal training or race speed i.e. swimming with fins or being pulled by a rope.

Assisted Training: Any type of training that helps the swimmer to go faster i.e. swimming with fins or being pulled by a rope or bungee cord.

B

B/C: An abbreviation for backstroke.

B/S: An abbreviation for breaststroke.

Back End Scull: A scull which focuses on the last part of the stroke before it enters the recovery phase.

Backstroke Turn Flags: Flags that are suspended across the width of the pool, 5m from the pool end to indicate to swimmers during backstroke, that the pool end is approaching assist backstroke swimmers to gauge their turn.

Back-Up Time: The manual time which is given to a swimmer if they fail to stop the electronic timing system by not touching the timing pad hard enough or the pad fails to record a time.

BC: An abbreviation for Backstroke.

Beats Per Minute (BPM): The number of times that a swimmer's heartbeat per over one minute.

Best Stroke: see Main Stroke

Bilateral Breathing: A breathing pattern requiring the swimmer to breathe on both sides of their body, while swimming freestyle.

Blocks see Starting Blocks

Boxes: The place at galas/meets where entry cards must be handed in before the start of the warm-up.

BPM: An abbreviation for Beats Per Minute (Heart Rate)

BR: An abbreviation for breaststroke

Breakout: The transition from exiting underwater to the surface, from either a dive or turn into the full stroke.

Breath Control: Sometimes called 'hypoxia training' which limits the number of breaths a swimmer can take.

Broken Swims: Training sets usually in two parts, an intense phase and a recovery phase. i.e. 4 x 150m as: 100m target times PB + 15 Seconds on 2.00, 50m O/C recovery on 1.00

BS: AN abbreviation for Breaststroke.

Builds: A training set, which requires the swimmer to start at a slow pace, and then gradually 'builds' speed into the swim.

C

Call Room see Whipping Area

Carbohydrates: The main source of energy found in foods such as pasta and potatoes, that should be a large part of a swimmer's diet.

Catch: The part of an arm stroke where the swimmer's hand enters the water and 'anchors' their hand in position before they start to pull/scull at the front end of the stroke.

Chlorine: The chemical used in most swimming pools to kill germs and bacteria and help keep the water clean, clear and safe in which to swim.

Closing Date: The date when entries for a competition have to be received either by its organiser or the club's gala/meet secretary.

Club Championship: Premier internal club competition usually open to all members.

Conversion Times: Swimming times usually converted from short course to long course.

Core strength: A swimmer's core is the muscles in their abdomen, hips and lower back. These are developed to provide the swimmer better streamlining, power, endurance and range of movement.

Cross Training: Any type of training outside of the water, that compliments a swimmer's training programme.

D

Deck: see Poolside

Dehydration: The depletion of body fluids, usually caused by swimmers not drinking enough during training or competition. This is the most common cause of swimmers getting cramp and headaches.

Descending: Training set or rep on reducing times. Requiring a faster swim.

Development Gala/Meet: A gala/meet, to develop a swimmer's competition experience.

Did Not Compete (DNC): The initials used to indicate a swimmer who failed to compete in an event.

Did Not Finnish (DNF): The initials used to indicate a swimmer who failed to finish their event.

Did Not Start (DNS): The initial used to indicate a swimmer who did not start an event.

Disqualification Codes: These are codes used by gala/meet officials to indicate why and when an infringement of the rules has taken place, resulting in the swimmer's subsequent disqualification.

Disqualified (DQ): A swimmer is disqualified because, in the opinion of a poolside/deck official, they have infringed on the rules.

Distance per stroke: The amount of distance a swimmer covers during one complete stroke.

Diving Pit: A separate pool or a pool set off to the side of the competition pool. This pool has deeper water than a standard swimming pool, with diving boards/platforms. During a meet, this area may be designated as a swim-down pool.

DNC: see Did Not Compete

DNF: see Did Not Finish

DNS: see Did Not Start

Dolphin Kick: A kicking action used in butterfly, where the swimmer kicks with straight legs placed together.

Dorsiflexion: The foot position where it is flexed toward the front of the leg.

Double Arm Pull: A drill where the swimmer performs a pulling action with both arms pulling simultaneously.

Down sweep: see Sweep

DPS: An abbreviation for distance per stroke

DQ: see Disqualified

Drafting: Swimming behind another swimmer, to save energy. This technique is used frequently in open water swimming.

Drag: The resistance caused by the swimmer's head, body or limbs, as they move through the water

Drill Pace: A slow, smooth and steady swimming pace, to enable the swimmer to recover and/or learn/concentrate on their technique.

Drill: A series of exercises, drills and activities, used to develop a swimmer's stroke which focuses on a particular stroke and/or particular aspects of the stroke.

Dropped Time: When a swimmer goes faster than the previous performance they have 'dropped their time' or performed a personal best time.

Dryland Training: See Land Training

Dual Clubbing: Where a swimmer, usually due to educational commitments, swims for two clubs. One at or near their educational establishment and the second club is usually their original 'hometown' swimming club.

Dynamic Stretching: The type of stretching which requires the swimmer to stretch while performing full 'swinging' motions.

E

Easy & Smooth: Performing a swimming activity using minimum effort and with a great technique.

Easy: Performing a swimming activity using minimum effort.

EBP: Event Best Performance see Event Best Time.

EBT see Event Best Time.

Electronic Timing: A timing system which is operated electronically and linked to the touchpads in the water at the end of each lane. Most systems are linked to a scoreboard that displays the swimmer's times.

Entry Cards A swimmer receives an entry card from a competition organiser for each event that they have successfully applied. On arrival at the competition venue, the swimmer is required to 'post' these cards in a box to confirm their acceptance of their participation in relevant events.

Entry Deadline: A date when entries must be handed into either the host club or the club's competition secretary.

Entry Fees: The amount a swimmer is charged to enter an event. This fee varies from meet to meet.

Entry Limit: Each gala/meet may have a limit on the number of swimmers they can accept.

Entry Time: The event entry time a swimmer provides when applying to enter a competition.

Even Split: When a swimmer swims at an even pace during training or competition.

Evens: Reps within a set with even numbers.

Event Best Time: The best time recorded at a particular event, normally at an annual championship or gala.

Exit Phase: The phase of the arm stroke, after the pull phase and before the recovery phase, where the swimmer's hand leaves the water.

F

F/S: An abbreviation for freestyle.

False Start: Occurs when a swimmer leaves the starting block or is moving on the block before the starter starts the race. The swimmer will be disqualified for making a false start.

False Start Rope: **see Recall Rope**

Fartlek: 'Speed Play' a series of training swims at a varying pace, slow, medium and fast etc.

Fat: A source of food energy that should be a small part of a swimmer's diet.

Faulty Start: Occurs when a swimmer/s leaves the starting block due to an error of an official or failure of the starting equipment. Swimmer/s should not be disqualified in these instances.

File: A group of swimmers, swimming in a line, either in the same lane or on the same side of the lane.

Flexion: Bending of a limb or joint.

Flip turn: see Tumble Turn

Flutter Kick: A kicking action used in both Freestyle and Backstroke, where the swimmer kicks alternately with a straight leg kick.

Fly: An abbreviation for butterfly.

Foot Flexion: There are two types of foot flexion: pointing your foot (plantar flexion) and flexing it upwards (dorsiflexion).

Form Stroke: A collective term for either backstroke, breaststroke or butterfly.

Front Crawl: Another name used for freestyle.

Front End: A scull or drill performed at or to simulate the first part of the stroke.

FS: An abbreviation for freestyle.

G

Gala: A swimming competition

Goals: Short, medium and long-range aims & objectives set by swimmers at the start of each season and agreed by the coaches.

Grab Start: A start where the swimmer places their feet in a parallel position on the blocks.

H

Hand Timing: Timing system operated manually, by the use of stopwatches.

HDW see Heat Declared Winner

Heart Rate Training: Training set where the swimmer is controlled by heart rate levels.

Heat Declared Winner (HDW) Commonly used in galas/open meets with a large entry list and schedule, where heats are arranged with swimmers seeded by their entry times. Once all the heats have been completed, the placings for each age group are calculated from the times recorded.

Heats: A race held at a competition, usually consisting of swimmers with similar submitted entry times.

High-Velocity Overload: Training swimming part of the length/lap (no more than 15m) at full speed without breathing, rest of the set distance swim easy

HR: An abbreviation of heart rate

HRT: An abbreviation of heart rate

HVO: An abbreviation of High-Velocity Overload

Hypertrophy: The increase in the size of organs (i.e. the heart) due to training.

Hypoxia Training see Breath Control

I
I.M. Order: The stroke order of an individual medley – butterfly, backstroke, breaststroke and freestyle.

I.M.: An abbreviation for Individual Medley.

In sweep: see Sweep

L
Ladder Swims: see Pyramid Swims

Land Training: Training conducted out of the water to gain additional benefits beyond those which can be achieved by training in the water alone. These include increased power, strength, endurance, speed, and coordination.

Lane Line: see Lane Rope

Lane Rope: The rope with floating markers that separate the individual swimming lanes.

Lap: see length.

Late Entries: Meet entries from a club or individual that are received by the meet host after the entry deadline. These entries are usually not accepted and are returned to the sender.

Lateral Position: Body and/or head position on the side.

Length: A single length (lap) of a pool is 'there and back' usually 25m or 50m

Lesson Plan: The plan formulated by the coach as a guide to objectives of a swimming session. It details the sets and drills to be performed during a training session.

Logbook/Swimming Log: A journal/diary/log for keeping all the swimmers important swimming documentation in one place. Used for storing documentation such as goal setting sheets, recording training and competition performance evaluation sheets. This is an important monitoring system to aid a swimmer's development and should be kept by the swimmer and reviewed periodically by the Coach.

Long Bungee: Two bungees joined lengthwise, one end attached to the web belt, the other to a secure fixing.

Long Course: Competitions held in a 50m pool

M

Macrocycle: A training period of some 15 to 24 weeks, usually with a goal at the end of each cycle.

Main Set: The primary training set within a training session, focusing on the session's objectives.

Main Stroke: The swimmer's best stroke, sometimes referred to as their 'number 1' stroke.

Manual Time: The time for a swim recorded manually by a timekeeper using a stopwatch.

Marshalling Area: see Whipping Area

Masters Swimmers: Swimmers usually over 19 years old, who have their own dedicated training sessions and compete in their own dedicated competitions.

Maximum Distance per Stroke: A drill/drill, to develop a long, smooth stroke to develop stroke length.

MDPS: An abbreviation for Maximum Distance Per Stroke

Meet: see Gala

Mesocycle: A training period of some 1 to 6 weeks normally with its own training emphasis and objectives.

Microcycle: A short training period with its own training emphasis and objectives.

Midpoint: A scull or drill performed at or to simulate the middle part of the stroke.

Mins: An abbreviation for minutes.

Monitoring: Performed by coaches when either observing, recording or evaluating a swimmer's performance or technique in training and/or competition.

Monthly Training Plan: An outlined plan of the month's training activities and objectives.

N

National Qualifying Time: The qualifying time needed for entry to a national championship.

National Swimming Championships: The premium national

swimming championships.

Negative Split: Swimming faster for the second half of the set distance than the first half

No Time Recorded (NRT): The abbreviation recorded on a heat sheet to indicate that a swimmer's time was not officially recorded.

NQT see National Qualifying Time

NTR see No Time Recorded.

Number 1 Stroke see Main Stroke

O

O/C: An abbreviation for own choice

Odds: Reps within a Set with even numbers.

Official Time: The swimmer's race time, usually recorded to one-hundredth of a second.

One Start Rule: Most competitions use the one start rule, which means that any swimmer responsible for a false start will be disqualified and not given a second chance to start.

Open Meet: Events that are 'open' to any qualified club or individual, although there may be a qualification standard/time.

Open Turn: A two-handed touch turn completed for Breaststroke and Butterfly

Open Water Swimming: Swimming that takes place outdoors either in the sea, rivers, lakes or docks etc.

OT see Official Time

Outsweep: see Sweep

Over the Top Start: To save time at some galas/meets for freestyle, breaststroke and butterfly races, the swimmers from the previous heat, may remain in the water until the next race starts.

Own Choice: A stroke or drill of the swimmer's choosing.

P

Pace Clock: A large free-standing or wall-mounted clock with a single hand used during training to give the swimmers a start time for a drill, sets and rest periods.

Para-Swimming: The specialist arm of swimming that caters for all those swimmers who have a disability and wish to train and compete.

PB: An abbreviation for Personal Best

Perceived Rate of Exertion (PRE): A subjective scale of effort assigned by the swimmer and/or coach, after training or competition.

Personal Best - The best time a swimmer has done so far in a particular stroke or event, either in training or competition.

Physiology: The scientific study of the functions in living systems and their parts.

Plantar Flexion: The foot position where the feet are in a pointed position, which reduces drag and places them in the optimum position for maximum propulsion.

Pool Floor Markings: The lines on the pool floor indicate the centre of a lane. The 'T' at the end of the black line indicates two metres from the end of the pool.

Poolside/: The area around the swimming pool reserved for swimmers, officials, and coaches.

Progression: A series of drills which when combined, breaks down into a 'progressive' order to help complete a more complex task.

Prone Position: A horizontal face-down body position.

Propulsion: The force that moves swimmers through the water.

Protein: Found in lean meat, milk and cheese, they are one of the main building blocks of body tissue and can also serve as a prime fuel source.

Pull Phase: The propulsive phase of the stroke performed underwater.

Pulse Rate: A method to monitor heart rate.

Push & Glide: Performed in the water at the start of a drill or drill. The swimmer 'pushes' off the pool wall with their feet, and glides in a streamlined position, to commence the exercise.

Pyramid: A training set where the workload/distance goes up then down.

Q

QT see Qualifying Time

Qualifying Time (QT): Times are necessary to enter most open meets, and all county, regional/state and national competitions. Some competitions will have upper and lower limits on their entry qualifying times.

R

Race Pace: Training at the same pace as the swimmer would race.

Rate of Perceived Exertion: a simple but effective method of monitoring and evaluating the intensity of a swimmer's performance during training and competition.

Recall Rope: A rope suspended across the width of the racing pool that is lowered to the water surface to stop swimmers, in the event of a false start.

Recovery Phase (arm/s): The part of the arm stroke, executed out of the water after the pull and exit phases, where both the arm and hand are returning to the catch position.

Recovery Phase (legs): The part of the leg kick is breaststroke that brings the swimmer's heels up to their buttocks.

Recovery: A drill, rep or set where the swimmer undertakes a slow and easy activity to allow the swimmer to recover from training.

Regional/State Qualifying Time (RQT): The qualifying time needed for entry to the regional/state swimming championship.

Relays: A swimming event in which four swimmers participate as a relay team. Each swimmer swimming an equal distance of the race. There are two types of relays: A Medley relay, where the first swimmer swims backstroke, the second swimmer swims breaststroke, the third swimmer swims butterfly and the last swimmer swims freestyle. The other type of relay is a freestyle relay, where all the swimmers swim freestyle.

Repetitions: A group of swims within a set.

Reps: An abbreviation for repetitions.

Resistance Training: A form of training with added resistance, to build either strength and/or stamina. i.e. using bungee/stretch cords.

Rest Interval: The period of rest and recovery during training between a set or a rep

RI: An abbreviation for a Rest Interval.

Rotation: A movement of the body in a forward (tucked) position when performing a tumble turn, or sideways when performing full stroke freestyle of backstroke.

RPE: An abbreviation for Rate of Perceived Exertion

RQT see Regional Qualifying Time

S

S/C see Stroke Count

S/L see Stroke Length

S/R see Stroke Rate

Scratch: To withdraw from an event after having declared an intention to participate.

Sculling: A swimming technique, focusing on the pitch and position of the swimmer's hands and forearms in the water, to achieve propulsion.

Secs: An abbreviation for seconds.

Set: see Training Set

Short Bungee: One bungee with one end attached to the web belt, the other to a secure fixing.

Short Course: Competitions held in a 25m pool

Sighting: An open water swimming navigation technique. Involving swimming with the head raised out of the water.

Signing In: Required at certain galas/meets where swimmers are required to 'sign in' against each event in which they are due to compete.

Signing Out: Required at certain galas/meets where swimmers are required to 'sign out' against each event they wish to withdraw from.

Sinker: A teaching device designed to sink to the bottom of the pool.

Skins: A swimming competition swam as an elimination event over several rounds.

Spearhead (Final): The lane order for spearheaded finals is decided from times in the heats or semi-finals. The fastest qualifier usually swims in lane 4, second fastest in lane 5, third in lane 3, fourth in lane 6, fifth in lane 2, sixth in lane 7, seventh in lane 1 and eighth in lane 8.

Speed Endurance: To perform at near maximum speed for a sustained period.

Speed Play: see Fartlek

Speeding Ticket: Awarded to a swimmer who swims too fast in a time graded gala/meet and will not be awarded points or medals.

Split: A portion of an event shorter than the total distance that is timed. i.e. a swimmer's first 25m or 50m time is taken as the swimmer swims their 100m race. It is common to take multiple splits for the longer distances and are used to determine if the swimmer is swimming at the correct race pace.

Sports Medicine: The branch of medicine dedicated to sports healing, prevention and rehabilitation.

Sports Psychology: The scientific study of the human mind and its functions in sport

Sports Science: The branch of science dedicated to sports performance.

Sprint Training: Training sets performed at faster than race pace.

Sprint: A swim at maximum pace.

SQT: State Qualifying Time see Regional/State Qualifying Time

Squad: A group of swimmers of roughly the same age and ability who train together.

Squadron: A freestyle relay of usually 10 or more swimmers in each team, arranged boy/girl in each age group, with the oldest swimmer going last.

Starting Block: The raised platform at the end of each lane of a competition pool, use for all competitive starts.

Starts: The start of a training set, gala/meet, either directly from the poolside/deck or in the case of backstroke an in the water start, usually with the aid of a starting block.

Static Stretching: The type of stretching which requires the swimmer to stretch while standing still. i.e. when touching their toes

Step Test: A form of training 'test set' which helps monitor the swimmer's fitness.

Streamlined: The 'torpedo' position adopted by swimmers during a start and exiting a turn to reduce drag and achieve maximum speed and distance through the water.

Stretching see Dynamic Stretching and also Static Stretching

Stroke Count (S/C): Counting the number of strokes per length, to enhance stroke length and consistent swimming.

Stroke Length (S/L): The length in which a swimmer performs a single arm stroke.

Stroke Rate (S/R): The rate in which a swimmer performs several arm strokes within a given time.

Submitted Time: Times used to enter swimmers into galas/meets.

Supine Position: A horizontal face-up head, body and leg position.

Sweep: A phase of the propulsive elements in an arm stroke, leg kick or sculling action.

Swim Bench: A resistance training bench, use as a part of land training, with weights and pulleys, specially designed to mimic the stroke actions in the water.

Swim-Down: see Warm-Down

Swimming Log see Logbook

Swim-off: In a heat/finals type competition, a race after the scheduled event to break a tie.

Synchronised Swimming: A combination of swimming, dance and gymnastics, performed to music, competing either in solo or team events.

T

Taper: The resting process in training for swimming competition. As a major competition draws near, the swimmer will "taper" off the distances swum, to enable the swimmer to compete at their peak capability during the competition.

Target Time: The time given for a swimmer to complete a set or rep, which usually includes the rest interval.

Teaching Pool: A pool, usually shallow or with an adjustable depth, that is specifically used for teaching. Sometimes used as a competition cool-down pool.

Test Sets: Training sets where the results are recorded to monitor a variety of criteria including the swimmer's fitness and/or the effectiveness of the training programme.

Threshold Set: A high-intensity training set, to train the swimmer to raise their fitness 'threshold' at which they can tolerate larger amounts of lactic acid.

Time Graded Gala: A competition with qualifying times, which the swimmer must achieve before they can enter the event.

Time Trial: An event or series of events where a swimmer attempts to achieve a required qualifying time.

Timekeeper Timekeepers record the time for competitors swimming in their lane. The chief timekeeper collects the times from the timekeepers and reviews them with the referee.

Touchpad: The removable plate (at the end of the pool) that is connected to an electronic timing system. A swimmer must properly touch the touchpad to register an official time in a race.

Track Start: A start where the swimmer places their feet one in front of the other on the blocks.

Training Camp: There are many types of training camps for just about every level of swimmer, usually organised by the club, county, regional/state or national association.

Training Overload: A type of training which overloads the swimmer with a series of intense training sets. The aim is that the swimmer adapts to this type of training and becomes fitter and stronger as a result.

Training Plan: see Lesson Plan

Training Set: A block of work during training, usually containing several reps and focusing on one type of training activity.

Training Systems: There are two main training systems. Aerobic: A system that requires oxygen and Anaerobic: A system that doesn't require oxygen.

Training Zones: The different types of swimming training i.e. anaerobic, aerobic, sprint etc.

Transition Turns: The turns in an individual medley that transfers the swimmer from one stroke to another.

Transition: see Breakout

Transitions (Triathlon): The period of a race where the triathlete transfers from one discipline to another. Either from the swim to the bike or the bike to the run.

Triathlon: A competitive event which comprises of three

continuous phases, a swim, a bike ride and a run. Distances for each phase can vary.

TT: see Time Trial

Tucked: The position a swimmer should adopt when performing a tumble turn. Chin on the chest, knees on stomach and heels on bottom.

Tumble Turn: The competitive freestyle or backstroke turn, sometimes referred to as the flip turn.

Turn Flags: see Backstroke Turn Flags

U

U/W: An abbreviation for underwater

Underwater Dolphin Kick: Performed by the swimmer in a tight streamlined position, with a vigorous double legged kick from below the knees. Commonly used during starts and turns for all strokes.

Undulation: The wave-like motion with the body a swimmer performs while swimming butterfly.

Unilateral Breathing: Breathing to one side while swimming freestyle. This can lead to an imbalance in the stroke over time. (see bilateral breathing)

Upsweep: see Sweep

V

VO2 Max: Distance training sets where swimmers are asked to swim as close to their maximum oxygen uptake will allow.

W

Warm-Down: A series of pool and poolside activities used by the swimmer after training or competition, essential for a swimmer's recovery and important for avoiding.

Warm-Down Pool: A separate pool for swimming down after a competition, which is usually a teaching pool or diving pit.

Warm-Up: A series of pool and poolside activities used by the swimmer before training or competition. Essential to warm-up the muscles and stimulate the blood flow.

Weekly Training Plan: Produced by the coach and is an outlined plan of the week's training session.

Weight Training: Traditionally performed by senior swimmers, using free weights, but is increasingly performed using pulleys and levers, swimmers perform a series of weight resistant exercises to increase strength and power during their land training programme.

Whipping Area: A room or area used during competition, on or near the poolside/deck, where the swimmers assemble before their event.

Y

Year Age: Age-determined events are categorised by the age of a swimmer on a specific date, usually either at year-end or the date of the competition.

Youth Swimmers: Swimmers usually aged 14 -17 years for girls and 15 – 18 for boys.

Made in the USA
Columbia, SC
15 March 2021